THE LOVE YOU SAVE

Also by Goldie Taylor

Paper Gods

The January Girl

In My Father's House

THE LOVE YOU SAVE

A MEMOIR

GOLDIE TAYLOR

HANOVER
SQUARE
PRESS

HANOVER
SQUARE
PRESS™

Recycling programs
for this product may
not exist in your area.

ISBN-13: 978-1-335-44937-5

The Love You Save

Copyright © 2023 by Goldie Taylor

Hanover Square Press
22 Adelaide St. West, 41st Floor
Toronto, Ontario M5H 4E3, Canada
HanoverSqPress.com
BookClubbish.com

Printed in U.S.A.

In memory of the women who made me

Willow weep for me, willow weep for me
Bend your branches down along the ground and cover me
Listen to my plea, hear me willow and weep for me
—Billie Holiday

Remember the rain that made your corn grow
—Haitian Proverb

PROLOGUE:
HOW HIGH THE MOON

She stood in the backyard, looking up that sky with her fists planted on her hips, shaking her head at the rain she knowed was coming. The sun was up, though the clouds were scant and it was hot out. But her big toe was aching, she said, and that was proof enough of a storm not yet on the horizon.

The knees that used to climb dead oak trees were ringed in soft pillows of fat now and stiffened by what she claimed was early-onset rheumatoid arthritis.

Her skin reddened and glistened in the heat. Heavy beads of sweat dripped off her chin and her sleeveless polyester blouse wetted at her deeply creased bosom. She was duck-footed with meaty calf muscles, and her short dark hair was still done up in pink foam rollers and covered with a floral scarf.

She could smell the river, Auntie said, sniffing the air.

Stubborn as a stiff-necked mule and with the temperament

of a meat ax, Auntie Gerald never did believe in letting some-body else take your laundry. She was deeply distrustful when it came to other people's food and, for a good long while, she believed store-bought cakes were the work of the Devil. She wouldn't so much as take a piss in a stranger's house.

I watched her pull the still-damp wash from the clothes-line, unpinning the bleached white sheets and pillowcases and tossing them into a basket. She'd run the dryer, I knew, something she typically avoided in the summer months to save on the electric bills.

"Carry this on back in there," she said. "You take a bath last night?"

"Yes, ma'am."

She eyed me with a whiff of suspicion. I was eight, maybe, give or take a year, and reeking like a pot of congealed chit-lins.

"You cain't smell ya'self?"

I followed Auntie up the wood plank steps, lugging the basket through the screen door and into the kitchen where Grandma Alice was rummaging through the cabinets, rooting around for a cast-iron skillet. She discovered it in the oven, right where she'd left it to dry after browning pork chops and flour gravy to go with fried okra and boiled white rice the night before. She was my mama and Auntie's mother, old, maybe seventy-five, and forgetful. By then, her eyesight was failing, and her ropy veins snaked along her leathery brown hands.

"Cut that fire down, Mama," Auntie said. "Y'ont need all that heat."

Auntie hauled the wash down to the basement. Grandma Alice slipped on her eyeglasses, studied the flame, and let the skillet warm up. She went about frying thin strips of bacon to go with her butter-and-sugar-laced grits and toasted two slices of white bread in the oven.

"You ate yet?"

"No, ma'am."

"Here, take some of this bacon and get yourself some milk. It's some grits left in there."

I helped myself to a dollop of grits, mixing in a pad of butter and sprinkling on a full teaspoon of granulated sugar. As usual, the bacon was cooked hard and broke up like days-old crackers between my teeth.

"Bless your food, child," Grandma Alice said.

I quickly said grace and shoveled more grits into my mouth.

My mother's mother thought that if you looked at anything long enough, good, bad, or otherwise, you could see God in it. And, I suppose, I always did believe that. Though, I still don't know what He had to do with burnt bacon.

The rain came and went.

At some point late that morning, Grandma Alice and Auntie Gerald settled down in upholstered chairs in the front room to watch *The Price Is Right*. I sat on the floor between them, while Auntie folded the last of the laundry.

"It'll rain again," she said. "Just watch and see what I tell you."

SOMEONE TO WATCH OVER ME

1

In the fall of 1974, Mama packed us up and moved to St. Ann, Missouri.

I suppose that little, painted frame house on St. Christopher Lane was my mother's way of proclaiming her self-sufficiency. Despite its pea green wood siding, splotches of sun-scorched grass and unpaved driveway, with Daddy dead and resting in Greenwood, it was tangible proof that she could lead a neat and orderly life and raise three productive, law-abiding children on her own.

It was twenty miles and a world away from East St. Louis, where most of our family still lived. In 1971, despite having been back from living in Chicago only a few weeks, with a bit of finagling, Mama's name landed at the top of the waiting list for a new public housing project. As it turns out, Auntie Gerald and cousin Dot Brown were both on the East St. Louis housing authority board.

For the little while that we lived there, our two-story town-house on Duck Hill was Mama's refuge. Whatever little bit we had seemed to be more than everybody else. Mama had a Zenith television and stereo console. The wood encasement, which looked more like a piece of fine furniture, housed a record player and an eight-track tape deck. The green plaid couches she bought off the showroom floor in Wellston were zipped up in custom plastic slipcovers. Mama hung up pretty curtains, affixed an oversize faux oil painting of a ship to the living room wall, dressed our beds in colorful linens and kept the living room furniture wiped down with Pledge.

It wasn't long, though, before things on Duck Hill went from sugar to shit.

What used to be a working-class town started to crack and the projects were the first to crumble. My older brother, Don-nie, was beaten and left for dead. He was only fourteen when somebody found him unconscious with his pockets turned inside out in a ditch next to the railroad tracks.

Then Daddy died. And Mama decided she'd had enough. She wanted something better for herself, someplace where dead bodies didn't turn up in the alley and the paint didn't peel off the school building walls.

I remember the morning the moving truck lumbered over the gravel road leading to our house. It was early yet. Snatches of sun beamed through the purple-ribboned sky as Mama shoved a box of pots and pans into the back seat of her car.

Leaving East St. Louis sometimes meant pulling double shifts at the St. Louis Airport Marriott to keep the lights on and put groceries in the cabinets. Mama was a cocktail waitress in the Windjammer, a lounge situated atop the hotel, and often worked days in a restaurant off the lobby. It was a decent trade. The two-bedroom, with its outdated avocado-green appliances and yellowish shag carpeting, was less than a mile from her job. It sat on the right side of the block coming up the hill.

Unlike our old neighborhood, there was a certain sense of safety amid the well-tended lawns, pristine sidewalks, and glowing streetlights. There were good schools, clean parks and well-stocked grocery stores that carried fresh meats, fruits and vegetables. There were no abandoned, burned-out houses or trash-littered lots, or heroin addicts perched on milk crates, and the traffic lights were in working order. There were no unpaved alleys, rooming houses, or putrid-smelling stockyards. Here, children played out in the street with no worry of random gunfire. Moving meant fewer things to remind her of Daddy's murder. Had he lived long enough, I am sure he would have been proud of her. The way he died left a hole in her heart, I know, but it was also a reminder of the life she didn't want anymore.

Early that first evening, after the truck was unloaded, Mama drove us up to Schnuck's supermarket, where she packed a handbasket with a frozen pepperoni pizza, pouches of powdered drink mix, and a small pink-and-white bag of C&H sugar. I spotted a drive-in movie theater on the way, and Mama drove past Northwest Plaza, then the biggest shopping mall in north St. Louis County. I had never seen so many stores and bright lights. A Baskin-Robbins 31 Flavors and a dance school were tucked in a strip mall on St. Charles Rock

Road, and a county-run library stood near the turn into our neighborhood at St. Gregory Lane. I had never seen an actual ice cream parlor before, but that wasn't nearly as exciting as the palatial library. I pressed my face to the window, staring until the last corner of the building fell out of sight as we turned off the main road.

We got back home after nightfall. Mama slipped an eight-track tape into the deck and spun the volume on the O'Jays.

For the love of money
People can't even walk the street.

My sister, Lori Ann, passed out paper plates and Styrofoam cups, while Mama twirled in the living room. Donnie busied himself making a pitcher of cherry red Kool-Aid. I slid onto a vinyl chair and hoisted myself up to the Formica-topped table. My bony legs weren't long enough to touch the floor. I remember how peaceful it was outside, the pleasant sounds of crickets singing in the night.

Mama said she was taking us to new schools that Monday morning. While the news filled me with nervous excitement, Donnie, who spent the day sulking and lugging boxes twice his size, said he wanted to go back to East St. Louis and stay with Auntie Gerald. Mama was visibly annoyed.

"These hunkies don't want us out here," he said.

Mama got so riled up that I thought she was going to dive-choke him on the spot. I made the mistake of calling my mother "crazy" once and paid for it with a busted lip and front baby tooth that was already on its way out.

"Who told you that?"

Donnie didn't say anything at first.

"Look at me when I'm talking to you!" she shouted. "Who told you that?!"

"Nobody," he whispered.

"What did you say?"

"Nobody."

"Well, tell that nobody they can kiss my black ass!"

I picked at the thin square of pizza, afraid of what might come next, half expecting Mama to lay hands on anything and anybody who moved. She drew her red leather cigarette case from her pocketbook, snapped open the silver kiss-lock, and took out a Benson & Hedges menthol. She lit it and took a long drag, letting the smoke waft under her nose. She was still wearing the wedding rings Daddy gave her.

"Crack that door," she said, blowing out a puff, "and hand me that ashtray."

Plumes filled the tiny kitchen. I piped up and said, "What're hunkies?"

A roar of laughter broke out.

Then, something in Mama's voice changed. Dragging on the butt, she laid out the rules.

"Be in this house before the streetlights come on. You break it, it's gone. Stay out of grown-folk business," she said, looking at me. "And don't embarrass me out here in front of these white people."

It never needed to be spoken, though it frequently was, but the last of the edicts covered nearly every aspect of our lives. St. Ann was all-white, whereas only a handful still lived in East St. Louis, a bottomed-out township on the easterly banks of the Mississippi. The era when the stores along Collinsville Avenue downtown bustled with customers was long gone. Around the turn of the century, the streets near our neighborhood were home to white mayors, doctors and lawyers who lived in stack stone mansions with their little white children. "If you cannot get a job in East St. Louis, you cannot get a job anywhere," went the age-old adage.

It was now something to be survived. Leaving there meant we were moving up in the world. Even though I still spent most weekends playing with my cousins along the cracked, pothole-laden asphalt streets, there was an expectation now that we would be something larger than ourselves, something divorced from whatever and wherever we had been.

I missed my Uncle Ross. In so many ways, Auntie Gerald's husband was the man my father couldn't or didn't know how to be. When I was coming up, my uncle was a gas station attendant at Stevenson's Hi-Point Amoco on Skinker Boulevard. Albert Ross was the first Black man working the full-service pump back when there was such a thing, and a doorman at a luxury condominium building a few blocks down along the northern edge of Forest Park. Like Mama, Uncle Ross believed in an honest day's work for an honest day's pay.

If my father fancied high-end clothing, like Mama said, living beyond his attainable means, and making company with women other than his wife, Uncle Ross certainly did not. Auntie Gerald was a housewife and her husband enjoyed gifting her with practical items: a gently used car, a set of encyclopedias and good dishes to go in the nice china cabinet they inherited from Great-Aunt Josie.

I'd lived with Auntie Gerald and Uncle Ross, on and off, since early '69, when I was a few months old. I spent so much time underfoot that, naturally, I started calling Auntie Gerald "Mama" after a while. Auntie was quick to correct me, but given how much we favored, most people thought that she was anyway.

Mama was in Chicago then, hiding from my father and hoping to put together enough money to send for her children. She was forced to leave the three of us—Donnie, Lori Ann, and me—because she needed time to get back on her feet and build a new life that didn't include the man who threatened to douse her in lighter fluid and set her on fire. For my mother, the price of my father's generosity, the life they led together laden with fineries, had become too costly.

In those early years, with both my parents in the wind and Auntie Gerald busy watching *Days of Our Lives*, it was sometimes left up to Uncle Ross to see after me. With my older cousins and siblings off at school, he would post me up on the front porch while he cut the grass or tended to his rosebushes and set me on the bump of a tree on the edge of the unpaved driveway while he worked under the hood of his car.

I was three years old when Auntie Gerald discovered I could read. I had not been to school yet, but I could phonetically sound out the signs hanging in the Jupiter discount store up on State Street. Auntie figured I had to have picked it up from watching *Sesame Street* and other children's programs on PBS. Then came billboard and highway signs, old

Jet magazines and the leftover newspapers. To her chagrin, I was writing on every surface I could find.

Uncle Ross soon purchased a set of *World Book* encyclopedia and *Childcraft* books, with tan padded covers, gold lettering, gilded-edge pages, from a door-to-door salesman and placed them on a bookstand at the top of the stairwell next to Auntie's bedroom. I started reading them, cover to cover.

No bigger than a bloodless tick, I used to scamper up the red-carpeted risers and slide down the polished balustrade until my narrow butt hit the ball-shaped post cap. When I was allowed outside with the older children, we played in the yard until we were dirty as hogs and the sweat poured down our faces. The smallest of the bunch, I was always the last one to clear the screen door at suppertime.

Auntie thought it best to enroll me in preschool that fall.

"An idle mind is the Devil's playground," she'd say.

Kinder College, the city's first federally funded Head Start program, was housed in the basement of a majestic, stacked stone church near the intersection of College and Veronica Avenues. Every so often, a box truck, loaded down with government-issued processed cheese, dehydrated milk, and bags of beans, pulled up outside and people lined the block for rations.

I was a year younger than the rest of the children, but it wasn't long before I was splitting days between the preschool and a kindergarten classroom at a school across the road.

I have little memory of Longfellow Elementary, except that I spent a lot of time away from the rest of the class on a mat that reeked of mold and urine in the back of the room while somebody I assume was a teacher waved flash cards in front of my face. By the time Mama made it back to East St. Louis in late '71, Grandma Alice was teaching me how to multiply with kidney beans at Auntie Gerald's kitchen table. Months later, Mama proudly dressed me up in a white cap and gown for the formal graduation from Kinder College.

In the upstairs sanctuary, I kept complaining about my feet until Auntie Gerald made me hush and get in line to take pictures with the diploma. The patent leather shoes were too tight, but the glare in her eye was terrifying. I stood between two boys, holding the certificate, red-faced and beating back tears, wearing a scowl severe enough to ward off a pack of feral dogs. Auntie Gerald didn't smoke and cuss like a cowboy like my mama did, but she had an evil streak that even the Devil had to think twice about testing.

The house was still half-unpacked when Mama loaded us into the car that Monday. Donnie and Lori Ann went to Hoech Junior High and I was enrolled at DeHart Elementary on the corner of Wismer and St. Charles Rock Roads. Despite having been skipped from preschool to first grade the year before, my school records from District 189 in East St. Louis showed only that I had completed kindergarten. It was decided that, based on my age, I would be placed in a first-grade classroom until things could be sorted out. I was the only Black child in my class.

When the dismissal bell rang, I didn't know where to go. I had no idea how I was supposed to get home or where exactly that was. I waited on the playground, watching a row of big yellow buses full of bright-faced children pull away. With the schoolyard now empty and the building dark, I started walking up St. Charles Rock Road until I got to a convenience store on St. Genevieve. I told the white lady behind the counter that I didn't know where I lived. She called the police.

I was busy spelling my name for the officer, when I spotted my brother, Donnie, hotfooting it past a Rexall Drugstore on the corner. Apparently, I was only a few blocks from our house. I had been assigned to a bus and when I didn't get off at the appointed stop, my brother came looking for me.

After a few questions, the officer handed me over to my brother and said, "You keep out of trouble, you hear?"

"Yes, sir," Donnie said. "She didn't mean any harm."

"I was talking to you, son."

Our neighbor Mrs. Farrell came from the other direction, rolling down St. Genevieve on her bike. She quickly assessed the situation and asked, "Are you two okay?"

Donnie glanced at the little stout white lady on the bicycle, then at the white cop. "Yes, ma'am," he replied.

"You all have a good day," the officer said, getting back into his squad car.

I ate dinner with the Farrell family that night. A year older than me, Debbie Farrell had things I didn't have—nicer clothes, a chest full of dolls and a mother who walked her younger brothers and her home from school. I remember wanting the kind of mother who did the laundry, cut my sandwiches into neat triangles and baked zucchini bread. Mama was usually leaving or gone to work before we made it home.

★ ★ ★

Mrs. Farrell had three kids of her own to look after. Between that and making sure Mr. Farrell had a decent dinner every night after his shift at a manufacturing plant, she had her hands full. The entire clan of dark-haired, blue-eyed Irish Catholics lived in a two-bedroom house a few doors down from ours. The boys, Chris and Andy, shared the room next to their parents while Debbie had the fully finished attic to herself. When Mrs. Farrell gave birth to two more boys—Marty and Charlie—one after the other, Mr. Farrell built out more bedrooms in the basement.

I quickly became a fixture at the Farrell house.

She never had to say so, but Mrs. Farrell knew what it might mean to be Black in St. Ann and how hard it likely was to navigate its waters. Still some people, like the neighbor across the street, openly groused about "all the niggers moving in," as if they themselves—some first- and second-generation Irish, Poles, Germans, and Italians—had not been somebody else's nigger at some point. Police squad cars eased by our house regularly, stopping midstreet to let us know they were watching.

Born on the same day of the same year, my mother and Mrs. Farrell couldn't have been more different. While Mama always drove a new car, I never once saw Mrs. Farrell behind the wheel of anything that ran on gasoline. Her husband, Richard, always drove her to the grocery store. When he wasn't watching Walter Cronkite delivering the evening news or buried in the pages of the *St. Louis Post-Dispatch*, Mr. Farrell loved *M*A*S*H*, a popular war comedy on CBS, and reruns of *Hogan's Heroes*. He was a big man with a heavy dark beard and kind, river-blue eyes that always lit up when he saw me coming up his walkway.

As women, my mother and Mrs. Farrell were deferential to one another, neither wanting to step on the other's toes where I was concerned. Mrs. Farrell knew my mother's struggles and knew it meant she couldn't always be there when her youngest child got into mischief, or needed a hand with her schoolwork or to make sure I ate some vegetables. That included stuffing me with plates of loathsome pickled beets.

I sometimes tagged along with them to Mass. We always walked to St. Gregory Parish. It had ornate furnishings and large stained-glass windows. The services were solemn. Back at our church in East St. Louis, people regularly whooped, hollered, and fell out in the pews. But the congregation at St. Gregory sang from hymnals and the prayers were whispered. I worried that God couldn't hear them.

At home, Mrs. Farrell baked and decorated homemade birthday cakes in her tiny, crowded kitchen. She made sure we put our library cards to good and frequent use. A kind spirit, she was slow to anger and eager to teach. But having two rambunctious boys like Chris and Andy would even test the patience of Job.

Debbie, good-natured and quiet, was more dutiful than the rest of us put together. We were inseparable. We tried to bake pies with the half-rotten apples that fell out of Miss Fran's tree and put on plays in the Farrells' backyard. Her mother watched from a fold-out lawn chair as we hung a blanket over the clothesline and performed songs from *The*

Osmonds. I regularly spent the night in her attic bedroom, and we sometimes played school. Debbie was always the teacher.

One day, she looked up from the jigsaw puzzle we were working on and asked, "Where's your dad?"

Even at six years old, I had already done the social math and knew the stigmas that came with single parenting. I was old enough to harbor some shame about not having a daddy to teach me how to ride a bike or even get after me if I didn't behave. Then, too, I suppose Mama didn't want people to think my father had willingly up and left her alone with three mouths to feed. She needed people to know that she had been a married woman and that each of her children were born within the confines of a marriage. When questioned, she simply said, "I am a widower."

There was no such designation for children and telling everybody your daddy was murdered meant he was probably up to no good in the first place. There was no good answer.

"I don't have one," I said.

Debbie was immediately confused. "Everybody has a father, silly."

"Well, I don't. He died a long time ago."

2

Grandma Alice came by our house in Duck Hill every so often to look after us. She was doing our laundry the day I sliced the heel of my foot open on a broken bottle in the courtyard. Grandma Alice poured peroxide over the cut and covered it with a Band-Aid. She was good like that, sometimes making salmon croquettes and one-pot spaghetti with onions and bell peppers and liked watching *Rowan & Martin's Laugh-In* on television. If Grandma Alice couldn't make it by, we were largely on our own when Mama left for work.

Lori Ann, then around ten or eleven, was usually put in charge. She was the only one among us with more than a lick of good sense and Mama had a hard time keeping Donnie pinned down.

In '72, when Donnie was about thirteen, my mother came home early from work and caught him up the alley near the corner store, on Thirteenth and Exchange Avenue, puffing on a Kool cigarette with a group of boys from his backyard band. Mama waved him home, drove down the alley, parked and waited for him at the door with a broom. I watched him cower in fear, guarding his head with his bony chocolate brown arms. She chased him into the kitchen. Dropping the painted red stick, she balled up her fists and called him all kinds of little black-assed motherfuckers until she got tired of swinging at him.

I remember screaming, "Stop! Stop!"

Mama stormed past me, went upstairs, and locked herself in her bedroom. Donnie sat down on the linoleum floor. He stared off into the tiling for a good long while.

"I wish Daddy was here," my sister whispered.

"I don't," Donnie said. "Y'ont remember how he used whip me with that extension cord? I hope h'ont never come back."

"Don't talk about my daddy!" I shouted.

He got up and broke the broomstick over his knee.

My father's murder, in 1973, seemed to change everything. Early that summer, we went to Auntie Gerald's house over in East St. Louis for a family cookout. Daddy came by. He was wearing slacks, a multicolored, button-down leisure shirt that exposed his hairy chest, and his herringbone necklace. Daddy was a large man, at least to me, with fair skin and, at twenty-nine, his hair was already deeply receded into the shape of a cul-de-sac. His mustache was dark and full, drifting down to his chin like a pair of bicycle handlebars. It was Memorial Day.

He gave me a dollar and sent me two doors down to Miss Cherry's, where I bought a yellow kite and collected the change. Miss Cherry was blind and counted coins and bills by the feel of them, which she did well enough to cheat unsuspecting children out of their money. When he saw how little money I had left, Daddy sent me back down to her slatboard house, where she ran a five-and-dime out of her front room. Miss Cherry had no problem telling a four-year-old that she didn't owe her anything. That is until my father showed up at her door.

"Hold on, baby," she said, nervously digging into her apron. "When is your birthday?"

"July 18."

"Well, if I don't see you before then," Miss Cherry said, pulling a bill from her cash drawer, "happy birthday to you."

"Lady, you can't see nobody."

"I know who's in my store," she said. "And I can hear well enough to know you one good-looking man. Don't nobody ugly talk like you. You gotta be fine."

Daddy grinned.

"You might be right about that," he said.

"I know I'm right," she said. "I bet you got a pretty smile."

She forked over a whole dollar, apologized, and called me precious. With that, my father was satisfied. Daddy helped me put the kite together on the back porch, while Uncle Ross tended to the meat on the grill. We sat on the wood plank steps, sipping grape Vess sodas, and waited for a good wind to blow.

It was the last time I saw him alive.

★ ★ ★

Six months later, just before daybreak, Mama sat at the edge of her bed, clutching her pale blue housecoat as she listened to the transistor radio on the nightstand. A familiar, melodic voice delivered the morning news, confirming what she already knew.

Her husband was dead.

It was November 5, 1973.

They were separated and had been for several years, living worlds apart and with other people now, but he still belonged to her.

He'd been invited to a late-night poker game, but when he got there the house was boarded up. He was ambushed and shot four times in the head, at least twice at point-blank range. One bullet entered his temple, exiting the other side of his head. The police found him facedown in a slick of ice on the asphalt. He had been robbed of his coat and two gold and diamond rings were stripped from his fingers. The herringbone necklace and the watch Grandma Cat gave him for his birthday that summer were missing.

I remember watching my mother descend the stairs that Sunday morning. Her voice breaking and her body still trembling, she reached for me.

"He's gone," she whispered, grabbing me with both hands. "Your daddy was killed."

Even then, I knew what death meant. Our family gathered at Auntie Gerald's house on Tenth Street that evening. Donnie and Lori Ann sat stone-faced and listless along the carpeted stairwell, peering down over the grown folks crowded into the living room. Auntie Gerald called Eddie Randle & Sons to start the funeral arrangements.

"Mary Alice, the man say Cat done already had the body picked up," Auntie Gerald said, referring to my father's mother, Catherine. "What'chu want me to tell him?"

Mama buried her face in her hands.

"I'ont know, Geraldine."

While they studied the question, Uncle Ross hand-fed me dinner—a piece of fried crevalle jack fish and one-pot spaghetti laced with chopped onions and bell peppers left over from that Friday. I curled up in his lap. He patted my back until I slept.

Several months later, after the icy winter thawed and the trees began to flower, Mama walked into Ted Smith Realty, sat in a metal foldout chair, and signed the rental agreement for the new house in St. Ann. Mr. Smith freely admitted he'd never rented to a "colored" family before, but Mama had perfect credit and assured him she'd been on her job for five years and counting.

My mother made fast friends with our next-door neighbor Miss Fran, a white lady with red roller-set hair and a shouty Pomeranian, who talked like she had four sets of teeth.

The same couldn't be said for Mr. Altepeter, who lived on the other side and almost never spoke to us. He had a friendly fawn-and-white German pointer that was trained not to leave the yard. Chipper would get to one of the contraction joints in the concrete walkway on either side of the property and invariably stop cold in his tracks. I'd never encountered such a thing before, a dog with manners who didn't shit in the house. Where we'd come from, there were only two kinds of dogs: mangy strays that roamed the block or angry mutts chained up to a tree in somebody's backyard.

We were one of only three Black families when we moved in and, I imagine to Mr. Altepeter's relief, it stayed that way for a good long while. The Winstons lived on the end of the block and the Scotts, a large industrious clan of four chatty daughters and a handsome brother, were around the corner on St. Henry Lane. Mama wore the significance of being among the first to live in the predominantly white enclave as a badge of honor, not as an auger of imminent social change but rather an indication of our individual morality and earnestness. There were niggers and then there was us, went the contention, the good black folks who spoke plain English, worked hard, and could be trusted to do right, and then the others who lacked the moral fortitude to work for anything better.

We dressed up in our Sunday best to go to the mall, lest anyone think us out of place, and Mama never left the house wearing curlers or a head scarf like the women in our old neighborhood did. I was regularly chastised for going barefoot outside. Whatever we were then, shoes or not, it wasn't enough for Mr. Altepeter, who eyed my brother with suspicion.

Donnie regularly catcalled marginally pretty, apple-bottomed girls and soon bought himself a gold tooth. A few months into the school year, he quit the football team and dropped out to pursue his proclivity for smoking marijuana and downing six-packs of Busch in the basement. The first time he stole Mama's car, I thought she was going to put him

in the ground next to Daddy. After all, more than one somebody nearly met his Maker for getting crossways with my
mama, including her on-and-off-again boyfriend.

He started coming around a few months before Daddy was
killed. With a face like Al Pacino and an explosive temper
that lit up after a string of beers, Tony didn't seem to have a
job, at least not someplace where he punched a clock. Even
so, he appeared to have plenty of money and drove a nice car.
My uncle Willie's wife, Doris Jean, said nobody ever broke
into our house back in East St. Louis and Mama could leave
her Concord unlocked in the public housing parking lot because Tony was a "button man" in Eastside Mob. Doris Jean,
who everybody called "Killer," couldn't keep a secret to save
her life. Auntie Gerald said she had diarrhea of the mouth
and chided Mama for trading gossip with their loose-lipped
sister-in-law.

I overheard Mama telling her Tony had a family, a wife and
two daughters who lived up in Granite City. I suppose that's
where he was when he wasn't locked up or staying with us.
He had more last names than most people have pairs of shoes.

When we were living in the projects on Duck Hill, Mama
and Tony used to put on beautiful coats and fancy shoes for
nights out on the town. The Christmas after Daddy died, we
were showered with presents and Tony gave Mama a little
white Chihuahua. She named him Chico. They were happy
together, generally speaking, until they weren't. Neither of
them had the good sense to walk away when things were still
good between them.

I was four years old the year he moved in with us, and he was sometimes left to babysit. With Mama at work, Tony cooked a skillet of Hamburger Helper for dinner one night. After we scraped our plates, I was sent upstairs to draw my own bath and unwittingly ran all the hot water out. Red-eyed and wobbling drunk, Tony checked the temperature. It was ice-cold and he drained it. He went downstairs to boil roasting pans of water, presumably, so I could have a warm bath. It was only enough to fill it a few inches. Tony ordered me to get in without testing the temperature. I could see the steam wafting from the tub.

"Get on in."

"No, no," I said. "It's hot."

"It ain't hot. Get in."

I didn't budge. He flew into a rage.

"I said get in the goddamn tub! Get in now, you dumb little bitch!"

I can still see the red welts and the yellow blisters that swelled on my pale bony legs. My butt singed.

"You're about as stubborn as your fucking mama."

My cries echoed off the ceramic tile and cinder block walls as the water burned my skin. My brother busted in the bathroom door, nearly ripping it off the hinges, and pulled me from the tub. Tony dragged him by the scruff of his neck into the hallway and shoved him over the stairwell railing. Donnie went tumbling down the steps.

Tony was sitting at the kitchen table, nervously smoking a cigarette, when my mother stormed in. Still dressed in her work clothes—a white turtleneck, red leather miniskirt and knee-high white go-go boots—she and Tony got to cussing and fighting. The ruckus spilled outside, with Mama calling him all kinds of goddamn dagos, ignorant peckerwoods, and no-good sons a bitches. It kept going, the shouting and shoving and spitting, until Mama pulled a pistol and shot him. She nicked him the first time. The second bullet struck him in the lower tibia, just above his ankle, shattering the bone.

"Touch my baby again, gawd-dammit, and I'll blow your other motherfucking leg off!"

Mama walked back in the house, wrapped the pistol in a headscarf, got a stool and tucked it in the gap between the top of the kitchen cabinet and the ceiling.

When the police finally showed up, Tony was lying on his back bleeding in the snowy gravel alleyway that ran behind our house. Tony refused to tell the cops who put a bullet in his leg. Neighbors poured out into the courtyard to get a good look. With no witnesses willing to talk and Tony's mouth shut up like a clam, my mother was briefly questioned and released.

She sat up in the living room, watching Johnny Carson, chain-smoking menthol cigarettes and drinking until they started playing "The Star-Spangled Banner."

Mama finished Tony's last Stag beer and went to bed.

By 1979, I was in love with heartthrobs Shaun Cassidy and Robby Benson. I tore their full-length, glossy centerfold pictures out of *Teen Beat* magazine and taped them to my bedroom wall. I wanted to be like the pretty girls on the cover of *Seventeen* magazine, the ones with the shiny white teeth, feather-cut bangs, halter tops and milky shoulders and pencil-thin brows, in the checkout line at the supermarket.

Mama said I wouldn't get tall enough to be a model, so I dangled myself upside down on the monkey bars at Schafer Park hoping my legs would stretch out. I stuffed my training bra with toilet paper because my friend Stephanie Miller had boobs and I begged my mother to press my Afro out straight with a Marcel hot comb and curling iron. When I asked about getting braces, she handed me a Popsicle stick to chew on for my bucktooth. Gnawing on the brown sticks was about as effective as suspending myself by the knees on the playground.

I'd read somewhere about a medication that pediatricians were prescribing for children with dwarfism. When I asked my mother about getting me injection of synthetic human growth hormones, she let out a groan.

"You shouldn't believe everything you read."

I was doing a lot of reading then. Between trips up to the library and Mama's bookshelf, I helped myself to Mr. Altepeter's morning newspaper before he could get to it.

Mrs. Shepherd, my sixth-grade teacher, looked at my book reports, which went on for pages on end, and sighed. I'd been kicked out of the Challenge program for gifted children the prior year after I stood on top of my desk and cussed out Mrs. Johnson. The teaching assistant routinely gave me failing grades, made me line up behind everybody else and picked me only when nobody else put their hand up. Whether out of racial animus or some other thing, she'd acted like I was invisible most of the time. That is until I climbed on top of that seat and shouted, "I'm right here, you fucking blind-ass bitch!"

I was sent to the principal's office. I stomped down the hall and sat down on a bench in the hallway outside the main office. The lead gifted teacher, Mrs. Schaper, was mortified. I was scared I might get sent home, but instead Principal McDaniel took me to the school counselor. After several in-school therapy sessions, it was decided that I might be better off in another classroom that fall. Mama got the dismissal letter in the mail.

"You don't need to be in a special class to be special," Mrs. Shepherd said.

She was a tall Black woman who had been given the duty of educating a sixth-grade class full of ne'er-do-wells. She got after me when I crossed the line and doted on me when I needed somebody to tell me I was worthwhile.

Even so, she eyed me warily when I said I wanted to run for student council president.

"Good," she said. "You need something to keep you busy."

Miss Spiegel, the short round PE teacher with a bowl-cut who taught us about menstrual periods in fifth grade, agreed. Although, she said I had the maturity of muskrat.

To their surprise and everybody else's, I won. It was the first time, Mrs. Shepherd said, that a Black child had been elected head of the class. The gravity of that missed me. But, of course, I thought winning an elementary school election was the natural progression toward one day becoming leader of the Free World. There hadn't been a Black president yet, and I figured I'd be the first.

My older sister found me and the whole idea obnoxious. Now in college, Lori Ann didn't have to put up with me for more than a few days at a time. Before she went off to school in northern Illinois, Mama made her take me with her to every concert she ever went to and sometimes on dates. To my sister's dismay, I was right there dancing in the aisles and making a nuisance of myself when the Spinners, the Jackson 5 and the Commodores came to play St. Louis.

When my sister was home, we sometimes shared a bed and one night I rolled over and hit her in the face. She swore I did it on purpose, which I did not readily deny. The belle of every ball, she was a beautiful girl and sophisticated for her age. I, on the other hand, was a tomboy with wild hair and an even wilder imagination.

We were seven years apart and had never been close. I suspect that was because I had the temperament, if not the smell, of a billy goat and it hadn't helped that I often pissed on her in the night.

While I was busy imitating Freddie Mercury with a mop-stick microphone, sister got pregnant, dropped out of college, married her high school sweetheart. She moved out when she was eighteen going on nineteen, so I had our room to myself.

Unfortunately, Tony didn't stay gone. After we moved to St. Ann, he kept coming back, posting up in Mama's bedroom for weeks at a time before disappearing again. Once, presumably between stints in jail, he donned platform shoes, a silk shirt, and a black leather blazer, and took me to a "father-daughter" event in the school cafeteria. I didn't have the good sense to be embarrassed about that, but I imagine he was trying to impress my mother. I suppose she felt bad for him. The .22-caliber pistol was small, but efficient. The bullet that tore through his leg had left him with a permanent limp.

Notwithstanding the fact that my mama had once tried to kill him, it felt strange to have somebody sitting next to me who vaguely resembled somebody's daddy, especially since this one smelled like cheap cologne and dressed like Serpico from the movie. When it was my turn to introduce him, I leaned over and whispered, "What name do you want me to tell them?"

With Tony tending house while Mama was at work, I was generally left to my own devices. I didn't mind, seeing as he stayed liquored up and slept most of the time. It went on like that, Tony tossing back shots of Scotch and me making home-made volcanoes with baking soda and vinegar, until the day he caught me stealing cigarettes out of Mama's carton and came after me with a two-hole grommet belt. I saw him wrap the belt around his hand and took off down the street, around St. Gregory, and across St. Charles Rock Road. I hid out in the library. With no place else to go, I waited for the Bi-State bus to make its way down from Northwest Plaza. I lied and said I was only ten. The driver nodded, waving me on.

I rode through the Wellston Loop and into the city limits, where it turned into M. L. King Drive, previously known as Easton Avenue. Auntie Killer's second-floor walk-up apartment was a block off King near the corner of Taylor and Aldine Avenues.

She was the sort of woman who smoked on the toilet. Auntie Killer had a pitted face, chain-smoked filtered cigarettes down to their butts, and regularly tossed back whiskey shots and cans of Budweiser. I remember the day she married my mother's brother in a little church in north St. Louis. They'd been living together for as long as I could remember, and he was still married to his first wife, Maxine, until the day Auntie Killer put her foot down.

Auntie Killer was a self-taught seamstress and, when she wasn't drinking and hosting impromptu cookouts, she worked at a dress factory downtown on Washington Street. After she got laid off, she sold fried fish and spaghetti for a dollar twenty-five a plate off the back porch to make ends meet. When she laughed, her eyes bulged and her mouth opened so wide you could see the epiglottis flap shaking in the back of her throat. She was, to put it politely, resourceful, and my Uncle Willie worshipped the air she breathed.

Auntie Killer had a homemade remedy for every known situation and ailment. Mama said it was hoodoo. If somebody messed with her husband or their dogs, Killer would scribble down their whole Christian name, toss the scrap of paper into an ice tray, and let the gods deal with them. One time, after she caught a woman brazenly flirting with Uncle Willie at the tavern up on the corner, she pissed in a ziplock bag, sealed the lady's name up in urine and left it in the icebox for months. We stopped going over for fish fries for a good long while after that and Auntie Gerald refused to eat her potato salad.

Auntie Killer carried a pistol, like Mama, and a mother-of-pearl stiletto switchblade in her pocketbook. Between that and the menagerie of mutts in the backyard, it was rare that anybody said a cross word in her house. She had an attack cat named Samantha, a particularly vicious black Siamese. Auntie Killer kept Sam on a chain hooked to a clothesline so she could run the yard but not get close enough to eat any-body's face off.

I guess I was hoping Auntie Killer would burn one of those pretty candles on her dresser and pray on me, like she did over money and love. Auntie Gerald used to grumble about how she and Mama were inviting the Devil into their houses with all those candles.

"Keep all that up and your house gone burn down."

Auntie Killer wasn't studying that. After all, she kept win-ning jackpots with fifty-cent straight-box bets. She swore one time, after she cursed a man with one of those candles, that he upped and died. Uncle Willie confirmed it, but nobody took his word for it because his liquor always did more talk-ing than he did.

Uncle Willie was a clean drunk. Auntie Killer made sure his slacks had a crisp crease, his shoes stayed shined, and his goatee was neatly edged. But she couldn't make him take the toothpick out of his mouth or remove his brown-tinted avia-tor sunglasses, even when they posed for their wedding photo.

When I got to their apartment that night, I was red-faced and out of breath. The dogs started yapping as soon as I crossed the back fence line. Sam the cat hissed and arched her back as I jetted past her, and up the metal stairs. I rapped on the window next to the fire escape. Uncle Willie opened the kitchen door.

"Baby, what'chu doing out here?"

Auntie Killer called Mama at work while I waited in her

wood-paneled kitchen. I stared up at the Serenity Prayer hanging on the wall over the dining room table. Mama had one in her house, too. Ours was in the bathroom.

Uncle Willie pulled up a chair. He'd been drinking and, as usual, he was wearing his sunglasses in the house and there was a toothpick wedged in his mouth.

"You want me to talk to your mama about Tony?"

"No, sir," I said.

"You can tell me what's going on."

I looked away, sniffling, and smearing the snot from my face.

"Let her be, Byrd," Auntie Killer said. "Mary Alice'll be here after-while."

Tony was packing his bags when we made it home from Auntie Killer's house. I figured he'd come back at some point because he always did. There were no tears, no foul words and nobody threatened to shoot anybody. Mama didn't even watch him pull out of the driveway. She sat at the kitchen table with a cup of instant Sanka coffee, closed her eyes and took a deep breath.

"Your daddy would've knocked his teeth down his throat."

Soon enough, Tony returned and they were back to fighting, sometimes upending furniture, and hurling small appliances. One time, he punched a hole in Mama's living room wall, cracking the plaster and felling a faux oil painting. She chased him off with the pistol.

Debbie was staying over that night. We barricaded ourselves in my bedroom, waited for the house to go silent and crept down the hall. Mama was boiling mad and beating back tears as she scooted the sofa back into place, flipped the coffee table upright and swept up the broken pieces of Daddy's lamp. I spent a week trying to glue the base back together. Like everything else, it never quite sat right.

Their last fight was worse than all the others. Mama said they were driving along Woodson Road in the neighboring city of St. John. Tony was drunk and weaving in and out of traffic. Apparently suffering from short-term memory loss, he threatened to kill her, weigh her body down with bricks, and dump her in the Mississippi. She pulled her gun out of her pocketbook and aimed it square at his head. He suddenly softened and agreed to take her home. She never took her eyes off him, she said. And, despite his pleading, she kept the pistol pointed at him.

"Jesus Christ, Pumpkin. C'mon now. You're not really going to kill me."

"The hell I won't! Try me, motherfucker!"

Somewhere along the line, a scuffle broke out and she shot him twice. It was the second time Mama felt the need to put a bullet in Tony and he was still limping from the first. Soaked in blood, he hobbled into a nearby tavern, claimed he had been robbed at gunpoint and phoned his father. The police got involved and Mama was arrested. I suppose that was enough for the both of them and, by early summer of 1980, Tony was long gone. She was out on bail, and the charges against my mother were soon dropped when the prosecutor could not locate the victim.

Mama bounced back, putting on her fineries and spritzing heavy rations of her favorite Chloe perfume. Then in her late thirties, my mother was a glamorous creature who adored doubled-up faux eyelashes almost as much as Billy Dee Williams. She regularly bought her clothes at a consignment store out in Clayton where rich white ladies dropped their out-of-date styles.

When she wasn't working, she spent Friday nights at the Regal Room back in East St. Louis. The small nightclub was situated next to a liquor store on the corner of Tenth Street and Broadway down the way from Auntie Gerald's house. With Tony gone, my mother had a string of suitors. They flocked like flies that summer. Though none of them, she said, "had a pot to piss in or a window to throw it out of."

I didn't like the strange men in our house, especially anybody my mama might feel the need to shoot at some point. If it looked like one of them might stay the night, I went to sleep over at the Farrells' house. A woman's worth, Mama still seemed to believe, was tied up in her ability to marry and make house with a man who met his obligations.

Mama might have dressed like a showgirl and packed a pistol back then, but she relished living within borders, as evidenced by the stamps in her furniture store payment book. She despised chaos and rarely talked about the things that ailed her soul. At the end of a long day, she'd have a nightcap, usually vodka and cranberry juice, and drift off, still sitting up in her bed. I'd quietly disappear into my bedroom, leaving her alone with her troubles.

3

I did not know it then, but the world was changing around me.

In the summer of 1980, the newspaper was full of stories about the Olympic boycott, the presidential election, American hostages in Iran, volcanoes, and the miracle baby conceived in a test tube during a procedure now known as in vitro fertilization. CNN aired its first newscast, and we were one of only a handful of families on our block who had cable.

I was mesmerized by it all.

My godfather, Thom Puckett, promised to buy me a new bike for my birthday, and, by late June, I was still working out my end of the bargain. Puckett owned a Sinclair gas station on the corner of N. Kingshighway and Natural Bridge Road a block down from the Carousel Motor Lodge where my father had worked. One of the first Black franchisees in the country, Puckett was a legend around north St. Louis, and he always had five dollars for me when we stopped to fill up Mama's AMC Concord.

One Saturday, he asked what I wanted for my birthday. I was turning twelve the following month. He said I should make it something special. My old Huffy had a broken chain and the black plastic seat had split in the summer heat. I had been coveting a ten-speed I saw displayed on the lower floor at the Northwest Plaza Sears. If I helped him out around the lot, Puckett said, he would "see about that bicycle."

I giddily agreed.

Every Saturday morning, he put me in charge of cleaning the stockroom. I added up the midday receipts on his tabletop calculator and stacked cans of motor oil for "Uncle" Frank, the white man who ran his auto repair bays. There were windshields to wash for cars that pulled up to the full-service pump, but I didn't mind. Though when summer temperatures started hitting one hundred degrees, Puckett decided I'd put in enough work.

"It's too damn hot to have her out on the lot."

Weeks after Mt. St. Helen's spewed its lava, smoke and ash into the sky, Puckett made good on his word and wrote my mother a check for the bike. It was the most beautiful thing I had ever seen—a twenty-four-inch orange ten-speed with a black seat and matching vinyl-wrapped handlebars. My brother, Donnie, helped me put it together, screwing on the seat and airing up the tires with a manual pump. I rode through the neighborhood that Sunday.

I wanted everybody to see it.

I popped out of bed the next day and hurriedly dressed for

summer day camp at Schafer Park. I fished a pair of white gym shorts with red trim and a red elastic tube top out of the drawer. I pulled the bike from the side yard and jetted up St. Christopher, and over St. Genevieve to St. Williams Lane. The sun still low but already burning away the mist. My legs, even with the saddle lowered flush, were barely long enough to reach the pedals.

It wasn't far, maybe a half mile. In those days, a little girl pedaling over to a park alone was not such a big deal. I proudly parked alongside the gazebo and went off to play checkers and swat tennis balls with my friend Debbie in the outdoor racquetball court. We spent the day playing board games, stringing beads, and making colorful paintings with a spin art contraption. I set up a chess board on one of the picnic tables and played myself for hours.

Sometime that afternoon, I started the way home. Pushing my way up the slope along St. Williams Lane, clumsily switching gears, I felt a tug at my bicycle seat as I hit the top up the small incline. It was a familiar face—an older high school boy, maybe sixteen or seventeen. I remember he was wearing a black K-SHE 95 FM Rock T-shirt.

I was taken down a path that led to Hoech Junior High School and through the parking lot to a house on the other side of Ashby Road, just south of Tiemeyer Park. He pushed me through the door of a screened-in back porch, yanked down my blue-and-white basketball shorts, and raped me on the slat board flooring.

I was eleven years old.

I remember how the moon hung in the sky. It was still hot,

even at night. He was standing over me then. I could feel him there, as I lay on my back inside the screened porch, but I couldn't look at him. The top of my head hurt from banging against the back wall of the house. My body smelled like his smoke. His semen dripped from between my legs.

He'd tried, again and again, to shove his limp penis in my mouth.

"Suck it, bitch."

I refused, clenching my teeth, and rolling my head sideways.

When he was through with me, I glanced up at his dripping penis as he pulled on his gym shorts. There were visible open sores, several pockmarks on his shaft.

He turned and left.

I took the long way home that night, down Ashby Road to St. Henry Lane, to avoid his house. I remember the dark sky, the buzzing, winged insects that danced around the streetlights, the way the stars in the sky seemed to walk along with me. I was relieved when I finally turned onto St. Christopher and made my way up the block. I wanted to tell somebody what he'd done to me. But more than anything, I remember being afraid. Mama would be mad that I was out past dark, and I was worried about what she might do.

I stumbled up the hill, coming upon a man standing in his yard. He watched me walk past his little brown house and said, "Go home, nigger."

He was the father of a girl named Vicki, a single dad who drank too much and was home too little. I said nothing and kept walking. I'd lost my house key in the scuffle, broken from the string of yarn from around my neck, so I banged on our front door. Hoping Donnie was home, I went to the basement and tapped on the window. Nobody answered. I thought about breaking one of the small basement windows but, even if I managed to get inside, the interior door at the top of the stairs was always locked. I would be stuck down in the basement, which typically smelled like a mix of incense, sewage, and ass.

Dazed and wobbly, I made my way up the driveway and sat on our painted concrete porch. My panties bloodied, my arms and knees scraped, the pain seemed to come from everywhere. The thought of telling Mama what happened, the thought of disappointing her, brought on a rush of tears. I sobbed until my chest hurt.

My cat Lucky emerged from the hedges along the side of Mr. Altepeter's house. I called her to me, pulled her into my lap and plucked the bush litter out of her fur. She still smelled like the leftover sardines I sometimes left outside for her. It was pitch-dark out by then.

I didn't know where my bike was. I figured I would never see it again. I waited on the porch until Mama pulled into the driveway.

My mother didn't ask about the bike or anything else. She did not waste a breath on where I had been, why I had blood on my face and abrasions all over my arms and legs or why my hair was unbraided and strewn about my head. When I tried to tell her what happened, she stopped abruptly and said, "Get on in this house."

I flinched, afraid she was going to hit me as I passed. I

rushed to the bathroom and threw up, barely missing the commode, and pissed myself. I heard Mama's bedroom door slam. I lay awake on the sofa for a good long while, staring at the ceiling, until I finally drifted off sometime before the sun came up.

My mother was the kind of woman who did her crying in the dark. She kept her burdens and shames to herself, lest the world see her unsteady. She was disappointed now, in me, in us and in what we had become.

She'd moved us to the suburbs in hopes of something better than the projects. Those well-laid plans were now tattered like an old snatch of fabric. Her youngest child, the one who made straight As and brought home every academic award the school had, was now weeping, and clutching herself on the living room sofa.

The taste of sick clung to my throat.

I awoke to find her sitting on the edge of the couch. She was on the telephone, whispering something to somebody and promising to call them back later on. She set the handset down on the receiver and reknotted her headscarf, staring off into the distance, through the front window. Her swollen eyes darted, then watered. I watched the lump in her throat travel down her neck and disappear.

Whether out of anger, pity, disgust, or some other thing, I could not say right then, but Mama abruptly got up, went to her bedroom, and shut the door. I was alone with myself, again.

I went to my room, stood in front of the dresser, and looked at myself in the mirror for the first time. My sandy brown hair, still uncombed, spilled over my shoulder covering a cluster of large, bright red hickies on my neck. I pulled off the bloodied panties and fished a fresh pair from the underwear drawer.

Mama appeared in the threshold of my bedroom door with her arms folded as she scanned the room. She wouldn't look at me directly.

"Clean this room," she said, surveying the mess. "Take a bath and don't leave this house until I say so."

She never gave a reason but, at the time, I assumed it was because I was outside after the streetlights came on and I let somebody make off with my bike. Looking back now, though, I am convinced it was the bruises and scars. There was a chance somebody might see me, somebody like Debbie's mother, and call the county child welfare office. Mama had a rule: *Don't embarrass me in front of these white people.*

I used some toilet paper and the last of the peroxide on my elbows and knees. One cut was so long that it took three bandages to cover. I thought Mama might call the police to come get the boy who had done this to me or, better still, call up some people from our old neighborhood, maybe some people who did not mind going to jail, the kind of people she always bragged to my aunties about knowing.

"I tried to get away," I said.

Mama pursed her lips, turned, and left.

I could still feel him. The sound of his voice boomed in my head.

Hold still, bitch!

I'd kicked and screamed and bit.

Let me go! Let me go!

I wanted to forget his T-shirt, his curly brown hair and pimple-laden skin. I wanted to forget the way he smelled like spoiled milk and the open lesions on his penis. I wanted to forget the excruciating pain and the sound of my own screams. I wanted to forget the way he gripped my neck and forced his smoky tongue into my mouth.

But, more than anything else, I wanted my mother to shoot the boy who hurt me. I wanted her to march down and around the block, bang on his mama's front door and shoot him dead. It was clear to me then, though, that she did not want to know his name or where he lived or what he'd done to me. I knew then and there, as she walked in her room and slammed the door again, that it was something we might never talk about.

Days passed before Mama summoned me into her room. It was late afternoon and she already had on her wig and makeup. Mama's bedroom was her private sanctuary and, when we were invited inside, it was never for anything good.

I stood in the doorway as she spread out a bath towel to cover her white comforter.

"Pull your pants off," she said, "and your drawers."

She waved me onto the bed, situated the cloth beneath me, then spread my bony knees to get a good look.

"You're growing hair," she said. "Under your arms too?"

I nodded.

I flinched as she wiped me down with a warm face rag. A greenish snot mixed with traces of blood dripped from my insides and my narrow hips throbbed. A flap of skin, the labia, was torn in at least two places, maybe three, and there was an abscess on the lower right side that swelled over the perineum. The blister had, by then, formed a crust which she gently began peeling away with a pair of tweezers, allowing the reddish puss to trickle out. I was crying then, staring up at the ceiling as she methodically cleared the scabbing, letting the tears run down my temples and into my hair. Waves of irritation, a quiet rage flashing in her eyes. Her sighs were loaded with disgust.

The tears gave way to howling, as she pressed the pustule between her fingers and ruptured the pinball-sized mass.

"Mama, it hurts! It hurts!"

She kept squeezing until she was satisfied that the boil had been sufficiently drained, saying nothing as she cleaned the wound and rubbed it with an ointment. The gel was clear and smooth and, for once, it was something that did not sting. I took a sharp breath as she touched the open wound.

"I'm sorry," I said.

"You can get up. Go get you some water."

The towel was soiled with dots of blood and ooze.

"Put that towel in the dirty clothes. Get some clean panties and put your shorts back on."

I left the room, did as I was told, and returned with a cup. She handed me two pills—antibiotics I assume—and told me to swallow them. I remember the weathered glance as I choked them down. I remember the glint of anger and the baking antipathy she seemed to have for me. I could not help but believe that whatever happened, wherever I had been, had been my fault.

I lay down on the foot of her bed and watched her change into her work clothes. Mama was a classic beauty, her nails and toes always polished with the same shade of deep tan from Sally Hansen that matched her lipstick. The musky sweet smell of her Chloe perfume filled the room.

"Don't leave this house. Don't answer that door for nobody," she said, "and keep your legs closed. You hear me?"

"Yes, ma'am," I mumbled.

I remember the way she clenched her jaws and furled her brows that night as I hobbled up the concrete porch and into the house. It had been late, a good ten o'clock or better the night she found me on the porch, and no child, let alone an eleven-year-old, belonged out in the street. It was not the bike or being out after dark. It was, I think, in her estimation, what I let somebody do to me, the disgrace I brought into her house and hurled at her feet.

She slung her pocketbook over her shoulder and left, letting the metal screen door clap against the frame. Peeking through the living room curtains, I watched the Concord back out of the yard and turn down the street.

It was as if my mother tucked away the unpleasantness and moved on. I remember thinking, if not knowing, that I was on my own. Whatever fixing I needed was my wagon to pull.

4

In the freezer, buried in the frost, I found the last Swanson
TV dinner. I tore back the plastic on the pan of frozen meat
loaf and mashed potatoes and placed it in the oven. When
the stove didn't heat, I realized the pilot light was out again,
and I was too scared to stick a match into the broiler. I gobbled down a can of potted meat and some saltine crackers
and looked up *pregnancy* in Mama's copy of the Physician's
Desk Reference.

I thumbed through the pages of the big red book until I
found the section I was searching for. Between that and the
film strip I remembered Miss Seigel showing us in fifth grade,
I was relieved to know I wasn't going to have a baby. I hadn't
even gotten my period yet.

Auntie Killer called for Mama.

"She's at work, Auntie."

"Your mama said she was off tonight."

"She left with her work clothes on. That's all I know."

"You alright?"

"Yes, ma'am."

"Get you some rest, baby. Run that air conditioner and make sure that front door is locked before you go to bed."

"Yes, ma'am."

That night, I stayed up late watching television in Mama's room, gnawing on the last sleeve of crackers. The news was filled with reports of old people dying in the heat. They'd found a man dead in his house, hunched over an air conditioner that was out of coolant and blowing hot air. The city morgue was at capacity, and they were running out of places to put all the bodies. In some neighborhoods, the roadways buckled, and whole sections of pavement broke into pieces as the asphalt expanded in the heat. People opened the hydrants so their children could cool themselves off.

Armed soldiers from the Missouri National Guard went door-to-door, handing out rotator fans and pulling bodies from three-story walk-ups. Senior citizen programs, like the one Grandma Alice went to, doubled as cooling centers. Auntie Gerald said Pastor Hubbard even canceled Sunday services at Mt. Perion because the units were too small to keep the sanctuary cold enough.

I shut off the television and went down to the basement to smoke a cigarette I'd taken out of Mama's carton in the refrigerator. The house was dark when I crawled into bed and buried myself in the blankets, smelling like tobacco. I lay there, pain stricken and trembling, and sweating in the covers. I was unmoored. I belonged nowhere and to no one specifically. Chills shot through my body.

When I woke up the next morning, Auntie Killer was there. Mama said she'd found me in the hallway stuffing a bag of apples in the linen closet. I didn't remember where I got the apples, but when she touched me, I let out a loud scream, my mouth so wide the corners could've split. As I was crying uncontrollably and thrashing about the floor, my brother rushed in to comfort me.

"It's okay, baby sister," I remember him whispering. "It over now. Ain't nobody gone touch you no more."

Mama changed the bedding and Donnie had tucked me back in. Auntie Killer now sat on the end of the bed, rubbing my legs. She advised a cool bath, a few tablespoons of castor oil and some baby aspirin.

The oil left a dreadful taste in my mouth, knotted my stomach, and spurred an especially ugly case of diarrhea, which Auntie Killer called "the shits."

"Let it run on through," she said.

Mama gave me a cup of sugar water to stave off dehydration, again on Auntie Killer's advice. She forced me to drink another with flour mixed in, saying it would tighten my bowels, but I threw up the thin paste all over the kitchen floor. Mama wondered out loud if she should take me down to see Dr. Nash, my pediatrician.

"It'll pass," Auntie Killer said. "She'ont need no doctor, Mary Alice."

Auntie Killer had a cure for everything. Later that night,

as I watched shadows flicker across my bedroom ceiling, I wondered if she could fix what was wrong with me.

My birthday, July 18, came and went without fanfare. I didn't expect a party or balloons, or cakes like Debbie's mother, Mrs. Farrell, often baked. It was a Friday morning and Mama had to work. She left a Hallmark card on my dresser along with the ten-dollar bill and the nice letter Grandma Catherine sent me. That morning, I went down to the creek, found a dry spot on the muddy bank, and puffed on one of Mama's cigarettes until the smoke got caught up in my chest. Coldwater Creek, which ran across the bottom of our hilly street, was my refuge. Mama never liked me going down there. While she was quick to boast about how well I was doing in school, I wondered then if she'd ever really wanted me. Right then, I felt like an inconvenience, a child that came along too long after the others and kept her from the life she might have had.

We were strangers then, my mother and me, the bonds twisted and tattered like snags of thread. Something was broken, in me and between us. Her comings and goings were like an apparition in the night.

In my mind's eye, I saw myself floating just above the rocks and ripples. The bruises had begun to fade, and the bump on my vagina had gone down. It was crusted over now, though oozing from its edges and sticking to my underwear. Bathing was still painful. Sometimes, I closed my eyes, spread my legs, and tilted my bottom up toward the faucet to let the warm water wash over the wound. It was soothing. Nothing, though, could save me from the dark of our house or the warring going on inside my head.

That day, I decided to use the birthday money to buy myself a dessert at a Shoney's Big Boy up on St. Charles Rock Road. I left my bike leaned against a concrete bollard on the side of the restaurant. The waitress delivered the double-layered, square chocolate sponge cake with whipped cream and a candle on top, which I gobbled down. By the time I finished slurping the bottom out of an ice cream soda, my belly was rumbling. There wasn't going to be a party, I knew, and Mama was scheduled to work that Saturday. I was alone, but I'd gotten used to that. And, at least for the moment, while I sat by myself, eating that chocolate cake, my heart didn't ache.

When I got outside, the ten-speed was gone.

I never went back to Schafer Park. Debbie, who was already in junior high, was spending more time with girls she went to school with, girls with acne and boyfriends and slim-fitting jeans with colorful plastic hair combs tucked in their back pockets. I mostly stayed in the house for the rest of that summer, watching game shows like *The Price Is Right* and *Let's Make a Deal* on television.

When I told Mama about the bike, she shrugged and said, "You left it out there unlocked, so you must not've wanted it."

5

Mama started sending me back to East St. Louis every Friday. I stayed weekends, only to return late Sunday nights to get ready for school. I had been in and out of Auntie Gerald's house since the day Mama first took off up the highway to Chicago, but things were different now.

My mother's sister was a walking barrel of discontent and generally annoyed by anything that moved. Life seemed to weigh on her like a winter coat in a high sun. She was forty-seven or so then and in the throes of menopause. She ran the air conditioning units and rotator fans around the clock. Between the waves of anger and hot flashes, little could soothe her.

For her, I was another mouth to feed when there were already too many lined up at her kitchen table with too little to go around. I was expected to fold in with the others, do my chores and disappear into the woodwork.

Children are to be seen and not heard.

With her own children now nearly grown and in and out of the house, Auntie Gerald took in others who belonged to somebody else. She never turned anybody away; thus somebody's child was always coming and going. Because my aunt and uncle were, by and large, country folk, their screen door was always swinging open. Few of them, bound by blood, water, or something else, had any home training to speak of and it was up to Auntie Gerald to make sure they got some. She was a hard-nosed disciplinarian who felt every perceived slight like a slap in the face. Uncle Ross was the enforcer, doling out whippings with a leather strap to keep everybody in line.

It was a raucous bunch. When my aunt and uncle weren't home, I was chided and teased and baited until I was red-faced and crying or mad and dumb enough to swing on somebody. Surviving the crosscurrents meant making myself small, though there were few places to hide from the congestion and mayhem.

Staying with Auntie Gerald meant suffering through harassment from her daughter. Bug was sixteen or so, already had a two-year-old son, and had dropped out of school. She typically woke up pissed off, smoked a joint and floated through most of her waking hours. When she wasn't as high as the Gateway Arch, she was in a near constant state of war, not unlike her mother, chugging sour pickle juice, often goading one child against another, and then snitching when we fought like hounds in the yard.

When she was in grade school, Bug was teased for having

short coarse hair. She used to lure her tormentors down the street until they got in front of the house. Like clockwork, she'd throw the first punch, banking on Uncle Ross to make everybody else jump in it. Given the choice between my uncle's belt and bloodying somebody's nose, we typically chose the latter.

"One fights, we all fight," went the rule.

Every day whatn't a bad day. I spent most Saturdays getting into some manner of mischief. That included making homemade slime with Auntie Gerald's Borax cleaner. I used a nine-volt battery to set off fiery currents in a ball of steel wool. I found the chemistry recipes in a science booklet I'd swiped from the library.

"Carry that mess on outdoors, Goldie Taylor! You gone blow my dern house up!"

For the most part, I was numb. I wasn't getting over what happened to me, so much as I was tucking it away. Sulking and pouting weren't allowed in Auntie Gerald's house anyway, lest she give you something to cry about. I kept busy with my makeshift science experiments and buried myself in any book I could find.

Some nights, as the sun went down and the moon crept up over the horizon, my cousins and some of the neighborhood kids played outside on the asphalt. They jumped double Dutch and, when the traffic cleared, they held impromptu footraces down the middle of the one-way street, from the stop light at Summit down to the stop sign at Pennsylvania. Sometimes, the races circled the block, with one runner going one direction and the other headed in the opposite direction. Lacking the skill, the rhythm, and the speed, I usually watched from the front porch. I couldn't keep up, but watching my cousins hotfoot it down the paved road kept me from reliving the night that boy dragged me into that house on Mert.

My second cousin, Ronnie Lee's son Booky, came most weekends, too. He wasn't much of a runner either and jump rope, he said, was for "punk ass, poo-butts" and girls. His mother, Gwen, was a nurse who lived in Brentwood, an inner-ring suburb out in west St. Louis County, and staying with his grandparents for the weekend was a good way to keep him out of trouble.

When we didn't have any money to play pinball down at the corner store, it was Booky who came up with the grand scheme to cut slugs out of old roofing tiles and plug them into the machine. His older sister Peety caught us making counterfeit quarters with Uncle Ross's X-ACTO knife on the back porch and blackmailed us out of every piece of candy we had. Once, when we made off with a bunch of Hostess Twinkies and Cupcakes from the Nationals Supermarket up on State Street and the half-a-mustache security guard chased us down the street, Peety caught us with the empty wrappers and cream-smeared faces and made us take over her chores.

Anybody taller than a field possum had housework to do. I dutifully polished all the living and dining room furniture every Sunday after church and swept the stairs with a short-handled broom until Auntie Gerald decided it was enough. The kitchen belonged to Booky and me. It had to be spotless every night before we crawled into our makeshift pallets spread out on the living room floor.

Uncle Ross knew we were wily little creatures, and our idle minds were capable of almost anything. He took us to see the Cardinals play baseball from the upper rafters at Busch Stadium. We watched the Von Erich brothers sling themselves around a wrestling ring at Kiel Auditorium on television. When he wasn't looking, we snuck swigs from his stash of Manischewitz wine and listened to Richard Pryor and Moms Mabley albums in the basement.

Grandma Alice, who lived in an upper bedroom, was a deeply religious woman who didn't believe anything that wasn't spelled out in the King James Bible. She thought the world of Booky and me. So much so that the older kids complained we could get away with first-degree murder if the crime happened when Grandma Alice was around. One time, Uncle Ross caught me on the lower roof outside Grandma Alice's bedroom window. At Booky's urging, I was about to hurl myself off the side of the house with a makeshift parachute I'd fashioned out of a sheet hitched to my back.

"Red! Get on down from there!"

Red was short for Dirty Red, a nickname I earned from a fleeting sense of hygiene. Auntie Gerald, who always called me by my whole name, got fed up one night and ordered me into a bath.

"You smell like outdoors! Get your molly self on up there in that tub, Goldie Taylor!"

She got busy trying to make a girl out of me. I was required to present myself to her every morning to make sure I had brushed my teeth, put on deodorant, and was actually wearing underwear. She said I was getting too old to keep playing outside with boys and no drawers on.

"Before you know good, it'll turn into something else."

I didn't know what something else was exactly. Peety explained and, suddenly, I understood why Booky was allowed to roam the edges of the Known Universe while I couldn't go more than two houses down in either direction. In my mind, taking a bath every day didn't make any sense if I couldn't go outside.

Grandma Alice warned us not to eat chocolate before playing in the sun.

"It'll make you be black as me," she said.

Given time and perspective, the old wives' tale seemed harmless then. It was, however, indicative of the colorism that pervaded our family.

"The blacker the berry, the sweeter the juice," Bug proclaimed.

Auntie Gerald, whose skin was the complexion and toughness of a barely ripe peach, sniffed and said, "Believe that mess if you wanna."

When she wasn't forcing me into a bathtub, Auntie Gerald taught me the rigors of mending and cooking. She put me in charge of baking box cakes for church functions. I could make any flavor I wanted, so long as it was one that she liked. She was especially fond of German chocolate and coconut. We picked collard greens, snapped pole beans, and hand-beat egg whites and sugar to make a meringue for the banana pudding until it felt like my wrist would fall off. I cracked and chopped up boiled eggs for potato salad and soaked black-eyed peas in an oversize speckled stew pot.

Auntie Gerald had a rule about her kitchen. The cook and the person whose job it was to clean up were never the same in her house. I was glad to help since that meant somebody else would have to "bust the suds."

"God bless the cook and sorry for the dishwasher," Auntie Gerald often said.

It was a tight-knit neighborhood. The Browns lived in a prefab house across the back alley on Ninth Street and were related to Grandma Alice somehow or another. Her cousin Jimmy Brown drove a big car and was a janitor at the Ford plant. Dot Brown was a housewife like Auntie Gerald and often came over for bridge club meetings with plates of deviled eggs and cucumber petit four sandwiches, which Auntie called "white folk food" behind her back.

When I wasn't doing Auntie Gerald's busywork, I played outside with Dot Brown's granddaughter Pudding and Claire Caradine, the loan shark's daughter from across the street.

The Caradines were a big family, in number and size, and their mother, Miss Bryson, ran their two-story duplex with a tight grip. If there was trouble going on outside, the Caradine kids were rarely around to see it. Their father, John, who everybody called Mr. Rent Man, sat shirtless on his porch wearing bib overalls every day, sunup to sundown, waiting to collect his weekly payments. Back then, Mr. Rent Man was quite literally the only "bank" in town who would loan money to seed a home business, bail your son out of jail or pay the light bill. If you didn't pay him back, that was the

last piece of money he'd give you. He never had to go looking for anybody.

The Caradines owned both sides of their duplex and had
an old piano in the lower main hall that separated the units.
They churched every Sunday, like we did, and Claire was on
punishment almost as much as I was. I broke more rules, but
she had stricter parents, so the math worked out.

I was sitting out on the porch when that "something else"
Auntie Gerald was talking about rolled by on a bicycle. He
had sun-kissed, curly hair and bright brown eyes. Before I
could figure out where he went, Uncle Ross called me into
the house. The boy came back a while later to introduce himself. His name was Darnell.

Until that moment, I hadn't thought about boys—at least
not like this. I preferred the kind who couldn't touch you,
like Leif Garrett and Robby Benson, whose pictures used
to hang on my bedroom wall. They had perfect teeth and
perfect manners. They weren't the sort, at least in my mind,
who would drag you into somebody's house. Here was Darnell, alive and good-looking and nonthreatening, and my
heart just stopped beating. Suddenly, I was going to find the
desire to take a bath and brush my hair every day. In a blink
of an eye, I wanted better clothes, longer hair and straighter
teeth than I had.

As it turned out, Darnell was visiting his cousin Eric, whose
mother ran a candy shop out the back of her prefab house
across the alley on Ninth Street. He was afraid of his own

shadow, and he certainly wasn't going to put his lips any-where near mine.

"Goldie's got a boyfriend!" came a sing-song voice from across the street.

An older boy named Marcus, who stayed with his grand-mother and had complex mental health issues, kept singing and teasing until Darnell got embarrassed and went home.

"What'd you go and do that for, Marcus?"

"It's…it's okay," he stammered. "He be over here all the time. And you're pretty. He'll come back."

Willie Bee, who was paralyzed from the waist down after getting shot in the back and got around in a manual wheel-chair, came rolling up.

"He stay over in the Gompers," Willie said.

The Samuel Gompers Homes, a barracks-style housing project built around World War II, was four blocks away on Sixth Street. I knew Jerome "Doo-Doo Red" Killian, the boy who shot Willie Bee, lived over there, too. Willie and Doo-Doo, both around thirteen at the time, were playing with a gun when it went off. Doo-Doo never went to jail. But most everybody thought he'd done it intentionally. They said Willie Bee was running away when the bullet hit him in the back. His spinal cord was severed. He was hospitalized for months and never walked again.

The Gompers were off-limits, for good reason, though Booky and I sometimes sneaked over to Summit Avenue to watch the action on the basketball court.

"Does he come over here a lot?" I asked.

Willie Bee laughed and said, "For you, he will."

A short while later, a little boy named Boss Man showed up looking for Booky. He was wearing a dingy T-shirt, cut-off shorts and holey tennis shoes with no socks. A wide-eyed miscreant with pitch-black eyes and a shaved head, he used to build clubhouses out of old doors from condemned houses and hunted for spare boards and old roller wheels to make skateboards. He lived over on Seventh Street and, ironically, his name was Darnell, too.

While most of us had parents, or at least somebody to come home to, and rules to live by, Boss Man didn't seem to have any. There was no dinnertime, no curfew and nobody around to look after him. He was outside at daybreak and didn't go home until well after the streetlights came on. At seven or eight, he cussed and spit like a grown man. Auntie Gerald wouldn't allow him in her yard let alone inside the house. Sometimes, when he said he was hungry, she made him stand at the back door and handed him a plate to eat on the porch.

We went exploring the bowels an old burned-out house on Eighth Street that day. Booky left to go get one of Uncle Ross's claw hammers so we could harvest some boards to make a go-cart out of old skates. I was alone with Boss Man, and he suddenly turned on me, tried to shove his tongue through my clenched teeth and jammed his hand into my shorts. I pushed him with both hands, knocking him off-balance and into a pile of old boards, and took off running.

I sprinted home, dashing over Pennsylvania Avenue past Haynes Miracle Temple, a huge Pentecostal church known for the massive revival tent they pitched every summer. I cut the corner onto Tenth Street and shouted for Booky. My cousin and his friends, Jodie Peoples and Sean Clark, came running. I was huffing and crying by the time they got to me. Between breaths, I managed to tell them what happened.

Jodie, who was the twelve-year-old titular head of the T.A. Jodie Boys and known to swing bike chains and hurl bricks, promised to find Boss Man and choke the spit out of him. T.A. was short for Tough Ass, and Sean, a pint-size boy whose grandparents ran Haynes Miracle Temple, was an unofficial member. They quickly caught up with Boss Man, who wasn't exactly hiding. Jodie held him by the neck, dragged him back around to our house, and made him apologize. Boss Man threatened to bring his brother back to deal with Jodie.

"Go get him," Jodie said. "I'll fuck him up, too. You know where I stay at."

After the incident with Boss Man, I told Mama I didn't want to go back to East St. Louis anymore, even if it meant I wouldn't be able see the curly-haired boy who quickly became my "something else."

Mama dug her fists into her hips, leered at me and said, "You'll go wherever I say go."

By the end of the summer, Mama was caught up in the charms of a new man. L. C. Moore was a mountainous figure, around six foot six. He had movie star looks, slicked-back permed-straight hair, and drove a fancy burgundy Cadillac. Like Auntie Gerald's husband, Ross, L.C. was a Korean War veteran and was awarded a Purple Heart.

Ironically, L.C. was a homicide detective. He'd joined the police department in East St. Louis as a patrolman and stayed

for more than twenty-five years before retiring as head of the
city's homicide unit and moving on to the Illinois Department of Corrections, where he hunted fugitives for a living.

When Mama met him, L.C. was also the mayor's personal
bodyguard. Given the gaggle of pretty girls and corruption
allegations that tailed him, Carl Officer likely needed armed
protection. When he wasn't watching out for Mayor Officer,
L.C. pulled shifts as a security guard at Faces, a gay nightclub in downtown East St. Louis. It was a popular after-hours
spot, with multiple dance floors and drag shows upstairs, and
never seemed to close.

L.C. was a man with plenty of proverbial piss pots and
windows. Mama doted on her new boyfriend and paid him
a level of deference I had never seen before. She told Auntie
Killer it was love at first sight. I remember her glee the first
time he pulled up outside our house. I got a peek at his fancy
car. His vanity license plates, a popular thing back then, read:
TOP COP.

Back home in St. Ann, Mama spent most of her waking
hours either working at the hotel or out on the town with
L.C. I was alone again. The waves of sadness came back.
Stricken with grief, I remember the sound of my own silence.
Depressed and alone, I felt resentment swell in my bones. I remember thinking how ugly I was, how nobody, especially not
a nice boy like Darnell, would ever like me. I started plucking
out pubic hairs, a compulsion that would return in the years
since, and yanking hair from around the nape of my neck.

When my mother discovered the quarter-sized bald spots

in the back of my head, she drove me to a barbershop near Auntie Killer's house, where a man took clippers to my sandy brown ponytails and cut them down to a boyish Army-style Afro. When the barber turned me around to see myself in the mirror, I cried until I wheezed and got snotty.

"I'm bald headed," I said.

The barber tried to console me, as my mother looked on with her arms folded, gripping her elbows.

"You should learn to take better care of it," Mama said.

She never noticed the nicks in my inner forearms. Sometimes with a kitchen paring knife and sometimes one of the double-edge safety razors Mama used to arch her brows, I cut myself almost every day. The trickles of blood, the small cuts, were oddly soothing. I was in psychological distress then, I know, and actively plotting ways to take my own life. I am not so sure that I wanted to die, so much as I wanted something else, anything other than what was. I had given up on the notion that my mother would come home one day, hold me, and tell me that I was something good.

One night, I sat on my mother's bed and called Auntie Killer.

"What's wrong, baby?"

When I was afraid to talk to my mama about one thing or another, Auntie Killer was a ready and reliable go-between.

"I just wanted to say I love you," I said.

"We love you, too. You want me to put your uncle on the phone?"

"No, ma'am."

"You sure you doing okay? It's late."

"Yes, ma'am."

I hung up and burst into tears. I cried myself sick, throwing up until nothing but bile came out. I went back to Mama's room and opened her dresser.

I could see myself in her wide mirror, pimple-faced with a mess of unkempt, nappy hair. I remember thinking I was ugly. I took her gun out of her top drawer. It was wrapped in a silk scarf and tucked inside a zipped plastic bag. My hand was shaking as I picked it up.

I wanted to shoot the boy who hurt me. I imagined myself knocking on his front door and pulling the trigger. In my mind's eye, I could see the blood pouring out his head. I could hear the blaring police sirens.

Donnie, who had been sleeping on the couch because the basement was too hot, was usually watching *The Jeffersons* on television, cooing at girls on the phone or playing his Parliament and Funkadelic albums on Mama's record player to amuse himself. But that night, he was downstairs smoking weed with his on-and-off-again girlfriend Beverly. Music rumbled through the floorboards.

I locked myself in the bathroom and slid down onto the linoleum. My legs stretched out before me and my back against the door, I stared at the pistol and wept.

Precious Lord, take my hand.
Lead me on, let me stand.
I am tired, I am weak, I am worn…

It was the .22, the one Tony had given my mother, and I could see the circular bullet rims in the chamber. If I killed myself, I wondered if anybody would pray for me and sing for me like my cousin Bernadette's husband did when somebody died in the family. I wondered what kind of dress Mama would pick out and if she'd take me back to Mt. Perion.

I held it to my head.

The doorknob jiggled, then came a knock. Donnie needed to go the bathroom.

"I'm using it!" I called out. "You can pee downstairs in the drain."

"Girl, pull up your pants and open this damn door."

I wrapped the gun in a bath towel, flushed the toilet and cracked the door. Donnie rushed in, scooted me into the hallway and shut the door behind him.

I sat on my bed with the gun rolled up in a towel until I heard him go back downstairs. My twelve-year-old mind simply could not count up the cost of shooting myself in the bathroom. I didn't wonder what the world would be like without me or what my mother would go through. None of that mattered to me then. I figured there would be a funeral with pretty flowers and a lot of preaching, then they'd put me in the ground next to my daddy. Sitting there, alone with myself, I was mad that Donnie banged on the door in the first place. Now, I just didn't want to get caught with Mama's gun.

When the coast was clear, I put Mama's gun back in her top drawer beneath her panties and bras. Daddy's jewelry box, the one with the metal lions and studs on the front, sat on top of her dresser, next to a pink seven-day talisman candle she was burning to draw love. I knew Mama kept a copy of my father's obituary in the case. I took it and put it in a shoebox under my bed. With Mama off with L.C., I felt like my father and any record of his life belonged to me. I didn't want to kill myself because I had been raped. I was angry at the world for not giving a damn about it. At least Jodie was going to bust Boss Man in the mouth for trying to kiss me. The boy who assaulted me was still walking around our neighborhood with his hair blowing in the breeze, smoking weed with his friends, and otherwise enjoying life with no fear that he'd have to pay a cost for that.

My father, I believed, wouldn't have let that go unanswered. Still holding on to the ideal of who I believed he was, I resented the way people talked about him. I was too young to remember his drunken rages or the way they said he brutalized my mother and brother.

The father I knew bought me a yellow kite on Memorial Day and forced a cashier to hand over my change. He was the one who delivered thirteen Barbie dolls from my godmother, Goldie Holly, one for every year Mattel made them, for my fourth birthday in 1972. And, right then, all I wanted was to be with him. I waited for a good day to die.

On Labor Day night, September 1, 1980, after a family BBQ at Auntie Gerald's house, I swallowed a bottle of pills I found in Mama's medicine cabinet.

A SUNDAY
KIND OF LOVE

6

I started gagging and throwing up, hurling, and spitting Uncle Ross's BBQ and the undigested red-and-white Tylenol capsules into the commode. The sauce looked like blood in the toilet bowl. Bleary-eyed and unable to keep my stomach from bucking, I kept spitting up. It felt like my belly was turning inside out.

Mama came home and walked in right as yellow bile came spewing out. I felt my mother patting my back and I flung myself into her arms. She flushed the toilet, drew me a bath and sent me to bed.

"Don't go getting sick on me again," my mother called out. "I can't take much more of this."

"Just let me die."

"Girl, hush. You don't want to be dead. Ain't no coming back from that."

"You wouldn't care anyway."

"You really believe that? Here, if you don't think nobody care about you, take the rest of them," she said, jamming the bottle at me.

I turned away.

"Get your ass in that room. Don't come out until I say so."

I cried myself to sleep that night.

Time seemed to move more slowly now. One day indistinguishable from the last, I was in a constant state of unease. Grief-stricken and languid, I all but stopped going to school. I missed so many days that the district warned Mama that I might be held back.

Right around Thanksgiving, my mother said I'd be spending the holiday break with my paternal grandparents in south Florida. She already had the ticket and there was no discussion. I would be going alone. My bags were packed. Mama's large red suitcase was sitting next to the front door when I came home from school one day.

They were largely strangers to me when they left St. Louis for Miami in 1972. I had no real memory of them before my father's funeral. By the time I boarded a TWA flight in 1980, I had seen them only twice. There had been that fleeting moment at Daddy's memorial service and then for the Christmas holidays in '76.

A soft-spoken, genteel man whose sun didn't rise until his Cathy woke up in the morning, Roy was twelve years older. By my estimation, they married when she was in her midthirties. He was her second husband. A pensioned Army veteran and retired porter who worked aboard Southern Railway's

Crescent train from DC to New Orleans, Roy Jones was then a butler, and my grandmother was the matron at the same expansive estate in Coral Gables. They cavorted with the upper crust of Black people in south Florida.

Grandma Cat believed in dressing up nice to go to the airport and, as we made our way down the concourse, she began ticking off the stops we needed to make on the way home. Figuring there were no better clothes in the suitcase than what I had on, she told Grandpa to take us to Burdine's department store.

"You only have one chance to make a good impression," she said. "People will treat you based on who they believe you are."

She examined the fit of the tea-length dress.

"I need to take this in," she said, cinching it at the waist.

"The store can do that, Cathy. They have a seamstress."

"And no guarantee that it will be ready in time."

She purchased several new outfits for me, including a blue sateen holiday dress and two nice pairs of shoes, on Grandpa Roy's credit card. I was going meet their neighbors, my grandmother explained, and they were important people. Lawson Thomas was the first Black judge in the city and the first in all of Florida since Reconstruction and, at the time, his wife, Eugenia, was a county administrator. Decades later, the Miami-Dade Justice Center would bear Judge Thomas's name. Eugenia was the first Black president of the Florida Parent Teacher Association, and an elementary school was dedicated in her honor.

From the time they arrived in '72, together with the Thomases, my grandparents frequented galas and cocktail hours reserved for Black people who belonged to elite social clubs. Judge Thomas and Grandpa Roy were members of Sigma Pi Phi, known as the Boule, the nation's oldest and most exclusive Black Greek organization. They summered in Cape Cod and on Martha's Vineyard, and played in the annual North-South Tournament at Miami Springs Golf and Country Club. I discovered albums filled with photos from formal gatherings, most including the judge and his wife, who went by Jeanie.

"Thank you for the dress and all the clothes, Grandma. Everything is so nice."

"You're welcome, dear," she said. "Roy, pull over up there and let me get my dry cleaning."

They lived in a small, beautifully appointed house, situated on a curved lot at the intersection of Eleventh Avenue and NW Forty-First Street. Liberty City was still solidly middle-class then. Although, the fissures were already emerging.

I plunked down my suitcase on the living room floor and watched as my grandmother sorted through the hand-me-downs in Mama's red, hard-shell Samsonite. She bagged up everything that didn't meet her approval and tossed my favorite white tube top in the trash.

"We will send these to Goodwill. It isn't becoming of you," she said.

Grandma Cat was a diminutive woman with a fierce personality, and I got a full dose of it as she surveyed my broken clumps of hair. She pointed me to a dining room chair and demanded to know what happened.

"Mama took me to a barbershop and had the man cut it off."

"Why in heaven's name would she do that?"

I shrugged and lowered my head.

"She said I didn't take care of it."

She sent Grandpa to the store for a boxed hair relaxer and pulled out a pair of scissors and an electric curling iron. An hour or so later, when she was finished straightening, clipping, and styling my hair, I felt pretty for the first time. Grandma said I would be expected to attend a holiday party the following weekend and would need to be on my best behavior. She would show me how to curtsy, and my grandfather would give me an etiquette lesson. I needed to know, she said, how to hold a fork and polite conversation. She'd had elocution lessons herself as a child, she explained.

Grandma Cat then laid the comb down and said, "Tell me the rest of it."

I didn't want to, so she gave me a choice: tell her or let my mother tell it for me. My mother hadn't told her what happened to me. Grandma Cat was just pissed off that Mama had my hair chopped off and knew there was more to the story.

I started stammering and choking back tears as I told her why Mama had the back of my head shaved down. Grandpa was crying, too. He dabbed his eyes with his white handkerchief, then handed it to me. They traded nods and he got up to leave the house again.

"I'll be back before the game comes on."

The Dolphins were playing the New York Jets at the Orange Bowl stadium and, for the first and only time, NBC was running the game with no commentators and no microphones for the coaches or players.

"How are you going to know what's going on?"

"I don't need anybody talking over the game. I have you for that."

"If you say so."

After he left, Grandma Cat led me into her bedroom. I lay there in her lap a good long while, not talking, just sobbing as she stroked my cheek. Her terrier, Thorin, curled himself up next to me.

"Get it all out," she whispered, "because this is going to be the last of it. You cannot carry this thing around with you."

For the first time in my life, I told someone what happened to me in the back of that house on Ashby Road. I told her who he was and where he lived. I told her what he did to me.

"I saw him walking up St. Genevieve with two other boys," I said.

"When was this?"

"After school started back. They were pointing at me and laughing. I ran home."

"What did your mother have to say about all this?"

"Nothing."

"What do you mean nothing?"

"She didn't say anything."

"Did she call the police?"

"No, ma'am."

"What about Dr. Nash?"

I shrugged again. I was too ashamed to say anything about the boil and how Mama lanced it on her bed. Instead, I told her about the night before Halloween, when I decided to get back at Vicki's daddy, the man who called me a nigger. On Mischief Night, I took all of Mama's toilet paper out of the house and tossed it into his trees. I smeared the windows with potted meat and pelted them with eggs.

"Your mother told me about that," she said. "That man could have had you arrested."

"She made me go down there and clean it up."

I was talking in rapid fire now, recounting the night I tried to kill myself with Mama's Tylenol. I couldn't bring myself to talk about the first time when I had gotten within seconds of shooting myself in the head with my mother's gun.

"Dear heart, no matter what anyone tells you, there isn't any need in you feeling ashamed," Grandma Cat said. "There is nothing dirty about you, child. You are brilliant just like your father."

I took a long bath in her tub that night. When I asked about soap, she pointed me to a pretty dish.

"Not the fancy kind. The kind you wash with."

Grandma laughed.

"Honey, we don't have but one kind of soap in this house."

She handed me a floral towel from the linen closet. It looked like the ones Auntie Gerald hung up in her bathroom. Only nobody was allowed to touch them.

"Can I stay here with you?"

Her smile said she'd already been thinking about it.

"Miami isn't what it used to be," she said, nodding. "And I am much too old for that kind of thing."

"Please, let me stay."

She kissed the top of my head and said, "Let me pray on it."

★ ★ ★

When the winds suited her, Cat was a prolific storyteller. She'd wave her hands as if conducting an orchestra over the breakfast table, the bygone years unspooling like musical stanzas. She spoke of the beauty she had experienced in this life, the cities she'd seen, the world she'd known. One morning Grandma Cat beckoned me into the dining room. With Grandpa Roy looking on and sometimes ad-libbing, she launched into a string of stories about my father and their exploits.

There was that time, in 1965, when he was trapped in the Windsor Hotel, near Sarah Street and Lindell Boulevard in north St. Louis. Four or five armed men, to whom he owed a sizable gambling debt, had the building surrounded. They caught him counting cards at a poker house in the Central West End, she once explained, and they wanted their money back. In another telling, it was a high-stakes dice game gone awry. Daddy, she said, loaded the dice by drilling holes into one side and inserting small lead pellets. That, plus a controlled throw, made the white squares fall on their heaviest face.

Grandma Cat said the Windsor was locked down. The men questioned everybody going in and out of the hotel. Cat, who never told a story in which her only son wasn't the hero, said she hatched a plan.

She slipped on a church hat and a pair of house slippers, and stuffed an overnight bag with three loaded pistols wrapped in rags. At nightfall, feigning drunk, she stumbled past the men and into the lobby. Once upstairs, she gave Daddy the duffel.

Grandma Cat claimed that she and my father shot their way out of the Windsor.

After only a few days with my grandparents, I felt more alive than I ever had. I quickly settled into their daily routine. We took our meals together and Grandpa Roy always said grace. It had been a long time since I'd slept through the night and didn't wake up crying, and I was never left alone in the house.

One Sunday morning, we woke early for church. Grandpa Roy liked getting to the 9:00 a.m. service. St. Paul A.M.E. looked like Mt. Perion inside, only people sat upright with their hands in their laps and didn't so much as wave, let alone shout, at the preacher. Grandpa Roy called them the "frozen chosen." The choir sang from red books and were all dressed in robes. Every eye was trained on the director. Nobody clapped or swayed. The whole thing would've put the disciples to sleep.

After a forgettable sermon and some dry hymns, Grandpa Roy insisted on giving me a tour of the city. He took us over to Collins Avenue. There were beautiful hotels and open-air restaurants. Shirtless men jogged along the boulevard. I marveled at the Atlantic Ocean along Highway A1A. It was the first time I'd ever seen a body of water other than the murky Mississippi or a contaminated creek bed. Grandpa promised to take me to the beach.

"I don't have a swimming suit."

"You aren't getting in the water anyway," Grandma Cat quipped. "Too many sharks, jellyfish and things out there."

"What is the point in going if she cannot get in?"

"I'm not going to argue about it, Roy."

On the way home, we passed bright blue houses, some with pink flamingos in the yard, some with burglar bars and hurricane shutters. Detouring through the streets of Allapattah and Lemon City, a predominantly Haitian enclave abutting Liberty City, I realized my grandmother longed for my father like I did and that, in some ways, she saw me as his proxy, the things she'd left undone. When Grandma Cat said I reminded her of Daddy, she didn't hurl it like an insult as my mother sometimes did. In so many ways, my grandmother believed she had failed him. And she would spend the rest of her living days trying to make up for it.

On Christmas morning, I awoke to a stack of pretty boxes with my name written in cursive on the tags. Along with armloads of more new clothes, I unwrapped a pair of headphones, a tape recorder, and cassettes of music. I had no idea who John Coltrane, Billie Holiday and Sarah Vaughan were at the time, but I pretended to like them because my grandfather did.

That morning, over a breakfast of slow-fried bacon, poached eggs, and wheat toast at her dining room table, she leaped into another series of soaring tales. I delighted in the food and the formality of it all, as my grandfather instructed me on the proper use of utensils.

"Take it easy, dear heart," he said. "Never let anyone think you're hungry. Never scrape a plate clean and leave some drink in your glass like you expect another one."

Back home in East St. Louis, we routinely ate things like pig's feet and chitlins, neckbones, oxtails and collard

greens stewed with browned fat back. All of which I am sure
Grandma Cat would have frowned upon. Unlike Mama's
house, food was plentiful here.

Grandma Cat apparently didn't believe in canned fruit or
frozen TV dinners. She wouldn't allow me in the kitchen and
that meant I couldn't wash dishes. I should learn, she said, to be
a good guest. I regularly found my clothes laundered, pressed,
and neatly folded atop the dresser in their spare bedroom.

"I have to wash my own clothes at home," I said.

"And it shows, dear," Grandma Cat said.

"Mama works a lot," I said, "and she has a boyfriend."

I told her all about L.C. Grandma sniffed at the thought
of my mother dating, even if he was a detective and drove a
pretty Cadillac.

"Money doesn't make a man," she said. "Whatever happened to that Tony?"

"Mama shot him again. They were coming over Woodson Road. Mama said he threatened to dump her body in
the river."

Grandma Cat sighed and went back to folding laundry.

"She should've killed him the first time," she said over her
shoulder.

That evening my grandmother served roasted chicken,
mashed potatoes, gravy, and biscuits for dinner. She sliced a
fresh, homemade key lime pie and laid out coffee for Grandpa
Roy. It wasn't long before she set about telling more side-
splitting, eye-popping stories about my father and his exploits.
My grandfather gingerly interrupted to correct the record.

After dinner we stayed up playing Scrabble. It was Billie's voice that finally lulled me to sleep that night.

Willow weep for me
Willow weep for me
Bend your branches down
Along the ground and cover me

When the day had come for me to go home, I didn't want to go. I asked if I could stay in Miami with them. My grandfather grew somber.

"Cathy?" he said.

"Honey, I don't think it's the right time," my grandmother said.

There had been riots, she explained.

"I read about that in the newspaper."

"You read the newspaper?" my grandfather asked.

"Yes, sir. I read everything. It was on the news, too."

My grandfather laid his glasses down and peered at me. Cat took off her apron and sat down. This time, she let Roy do all the talking.

Earlier that year, in May, four Dade County officers were acquitted in the death of Arthur McDuffie, an insurance salesman and US Marine. Driving a motorcycle, McDuffie was stopped by six white officers and was subsequently beaten to death. The streets erupted, many believing there had been an orchestrated cover-up.

My grandfather was driving home from work with Grandma Cat when they encountered a makeshift roadblock.

Protestors had cordoned off swaths of Liberty City and Overtown. No one was allowed in except Black people, Grandma said. Drivers were told to put their arms out the window to prove it. Grandpa, a fair-complexioned man, attempted to stick out his hand when Grandmother stopped him.

"Roy, let me. You're too light-skinned."

Grandma Cat jutted her deep brown arm out for inspection. They were allowed to continue through the intersection. Another driver, a white man, Granddaddy said, was dragged from his car and his head was slammed with the cover of his trunk.

The McDuffie Riots went on for three days. In the end, eighteen people were killed and nearly a thousand arrested. Even months later, tensions were still high in the city and Grandmother said I needed to go home the next day as scheduled. I'd been there for three full weeks and school was starting back that Monday. She promised to send for me.

"Let me straighten some things out with your mother," she said.

It would be several years and another riot before I saw her again.

SUGAR ON THE FLOOR

7

By the summer of '81, the warring in my head was near constant. I had sharp memories about the day I was raped, and, at times, I awoke screaming in the dark. I was afraid to go outside, went days without bathing and rarely ate. My tangled, unwashed hair fell out in clumps. I don't remember crying or even talking much. I mostly kept to myself. It was safer that way, I thought.

I was scared that somebody might touch me.

Me and Mama were like ships passing in the night until the day I used a razor blade to arch my eyebrows. In a bizarre attempt to look like Farrah Fawcett, I also used a hot comb to straighten my hair and lopped off the front left section with a pair of her sewing scissors. I wanted feathered bangs like the white girls at school. I nicked my eyelid with the razor.

When she got home from work that night, she took one look at the blood trickling down my face, shook her head, and hauled off and slapped the daylights out of me. Cowering in the corner, I hollered out for my father.

"What did you say? What did you say?!"

"I want my daddy! I want my daddy! I want my daddy!"

I wanted her to hear me. I wanted her to feel my rebuke. I shouted it over, and over again, until she jammed her finger in my face and screamed, "Your father is dead! And he ain't never coming back!"

Mama was bleary-eyed and angry, angry that he'd left her and angry that I'd unwittingly hurled his murder in her face. She unwrapped a fresh razor blade, tossed the white paper, and tilted my head back. By the time she was finished, I had a few wisps of brow hairs left.

When I think about how small I was and how little I understood about the world, I admit, it's easy to be angry now. Trembling and scared, I wanted something different. Our world was full of slapping, drinking, cussing, and shooting. I wanted at least a pleasant house and a pleasant family like the Farrells had.

I cried myself to sleep.

One Saturday morning, Mama woke me early, told me to pack a bag and drove me Auntie Gerald's house in East St. Louis. She said little along the drive as she listened to the news on public radio. It was supposed to be another weeklong visit.

No matter how much time I spent living under my mother's roof, for as long as I could remember, the house on Tenth Street had always felt like home. Despite having paid every debt he ever owed on time, and proudly serving his country in the US Army, in 1969, Uncle Ross was Black and, thus, could not qualify for a bank loan. He was forced to take out a contract-for-deed mortgage, a high-interest predatory agreement backed by real estate investors out to profit off redlining.

Situated along the easterly banks of the Mississippi River in central Illinois, East St. Louis was once predominantly white. A massacre unfolded in 1917, ignited by labor disputes, when white people feared they would be forced from their well-paying jobs in nearby factories by Black migrants who emerged from the South beginning in the late 1800s. In the end, an estimated two hundred fifty black people were killed and approximately six thousand were left homeless, burned out of their brick bungalows and rooming houses.

When it was over, remaining residents picked up the pieces. The mayor pushed for reparations, paying white people for the property they lost to the fires and forcing insurance companies to pay out policies held by Black residents. Civil rights leaders came to town, mounting investigations into the massacre. But, otherwise, the city would go on about its business as one of the nation's most important stops along rail lines and barge routes.

However, white people began to abandon the city—first in trickles, then in droves as more Black people were drawn to its seemingly boundless economic opportunities. Between 1967 and 1970, nearly every remaining white family left East St. Louis for the suburbs.

Four decades before Uncle Ross put his name on the deed, the city lines were redrawn. The smokestacks and factories at the edge of town were de-annexed around 1926, so the companies wouldn't have to pay taxes into an increasingly

Black town. That year, the City of Monsanto—now named Sauget—was incorporated just south of town. National City, to the north, was home to the St. Louis National Stockyards Company. Industry swelled and, by 1945, it was called the "Hog Capital of the Nation." At one time, there were forty-three packing plants processing upward of one hundred thousand head of cattle and hogs a week.

The house sat well within sniffing distance of the putrid-smelling stockyards. By the time Auntie Gerald and Uncle Ross moved in, only a single white family remained on the block in the Exchange–N. Fifteenth Section of the city. Originally built in the late 1800s, there were three well-laid bedrooms, not counting the squat room in the basement, and a single oversize bath where Auntie Gerald hung up decorative towels that nobody ever dared dry their asses with.

When the expansive front porch could use a few well-placed nails or the living room needed a fresh coat of paint, Uncle Ross did all the work himself. Every Memorial Day, Veterans Day and Fourth of July, the man who once boosted his age by two years to qualify for military service on behalf of a country that didn't think he was worthy of pissing in a bathroom stall next to a white man or sharing the same water fountain, would proudly hoist an American flag into its place on the center porch pillar. He hung an English red cedar porch swing along the far-left end, suspended by cast-metal chain links attached to S-hooks, and planted shrub roses along the front edge.

When we got to Auntie Gerald's house, my cousin Booky met our car at the curb. We took off down the street toward

the corner store. There were new owners by then. The Co-
chrans from across the street rented the shuttered store, reopened it, and installed a Pac-Man machine in hopes new
customers might also spend money on overpriced cans of Vess
soda, single rolls of toilet paper, loose cigarettes and Red Hot
Riplets potato chips. They sold the spicy pickles my cousin
Bug adored so much from a jar on the counter and let her
have the leftover juice. Along the way, we passed a woman
sitting in a fold-out lawn chair on the porch of a duplex. I was
all at once alarmed and amused, if not insanely curious. Miss
Whatever-Her-Name-Was was buck naked from the "rooty
to the tooty," hooting and hollering like she was watching
some funny picture show that only she could see. Skinny as
a beanpole, her little brown children, one of them wearing
nothing but a diaper and a nose full of snot, scampered around
the yard while their mama's slack titties swayed in the wind
when she let out a laugh.

She caught sight of me and Booky, and hollered out, "Y'all
going to the stow? Bring me sumpin' back, hear?"

She disappeared into the house.

"Did you hear what she said?"

"Don't know and don't care," Booky said, "and you
shouldn't either, Go Go."

Plenty of folks had been hit running across Tenth Street,
which was deemed a state highway back then. I worried about
the children in the yard.

"Who's watching her kids?"

"What did I just say? Them her kids."

"Okay, but she wasn't wearing any underwear!"

At the store, we had to wait in line behind a twentysome-thing white lady, which was strange in and of itself. She was yelling at the cashier because they didn't have a business li-cense and wouldn't take food stamps as payment.

"This is money!" she said waving the stapled booklet in front of the Plexiglas window. "You out here breaking one law. Who gives a good got-damn if you break another one?"

We waited our turn, then bought a sack full of Now & Lat-ers, Chick-O-Sticks and Mary Janes. On the way back, I no-ticed the kids were gone and there was no sign of the naked lady or her husband when we passed again. The woman on the porch was an addict, I would later learn. We sometimes saw her roaming the block, making it up to the corner of Tenth and Pennsylvania before her husband, beset with the same addictions, took her home.

"Who was that white lady in the store?"

"You know they be tricking over in those apartments."

"What's tricking?"

"Hoeing."

"What's that?"

Booky chuckled and said, "Here, Go Go, shut up and eat a Chick-O-Stick."

We spotted Old Man Ford coming out the alley and took off running down the street. He haunted the numbered blocks between Summit and Pennsylvania Avenues, carry-ing an empty five-gallon paint bucket and a brown, sawed-off broomstick. He'd raped one of the girls from across the street and everybody knew he'd strangled Miss Cherry, the blind shopkeeper, to death.

He never made it to jail. Somebody said he was found dead in the alley behind the Sanders house. He'd been back there in the weeds for a long time, they say, the stench of his decomposing body masked by the odor coming out of the stockyards.

When we got back, Mama was gone. I was used to my mother coming and going without so much as a "hello" or a "goodbye," so I thought nothing of it at the time. It was a week or more before my mama came back. She called me out to the car. Dressed in her work clothes, she seemed to be in a hurry.

"Take this stuff in the house."

My clothes, stuffed into brown paper bags from the grocery store, were piled into the truck.

"How long am I staying here?"

"As long as I say so."

She didn't stay but a few minutes, just long enough to trade pleasantries with Auntie Gerald and hand her a check, which my aunt folded and tucked into her brassiere.

Even then, as my mama backed out of the gravel driveway, I did not realize what was happening until I overheard my cousin Bug tell somebody on the telephone that I'd been "dumped." I ran upstairs and locked myself in the bathroom. That's when I noticed my shorts were soaked in blood. The first full menses came on like a rolling mudslide.

"You so smart you stupid," Bug said. "Your mama didn't tell you nothing about getting your period?"

"I'm not stupid. I know what a menstruation is. I guess you do, too."

Bug was twenty and her son, Marceo, a burly stump of a

boy who everybody called "Fat Man," was five. She'd gotten pregnant at fourteen and went into labor a few months before her fifteenth birthday in 1976.

"Shut up before I bust you in your damn face," she said, sneering.

Auntie Gerald handed me a bag of Kotex pads.

"Here, clean yourself up and put one on. And wash between your legs real good. Don't get no blood on my floor."

I put the thick white pad on upside down, the adhesive sticking to my pubic hair. A while later, when Grandma Alice saw blood running down my leg, she took me back into the bathroom and gave me a new one.

"Stick it to your drawers," she said.

It was Uncle Ross, though, who took me into their upper bedroom and gave me "the talk" that night. He warned me about sexual contact during certain days of the month. Though he wouldn't say exactly why, it all matched up with what I'd read in Mama's medical book and remembered from Miss Seigel's filmstrip. He was very clear about how a young lady should comport herself in public. He admonished me to dress modestly.

"Keep yourself clean, Red," he said, "especially when your period comes on."

Although he was quick to mete out discipline with thick leather belts and sometimes a souvenir wooden paddle from an amusement park, Uncle Ross was a kind man. We all knew the fullness of his compassion and never once doubted his devotion to us. Just as he'd promised Daddy, he eagerly stepped in my father's shoes.

★ ★ ★

Auntie Gerald went to church three or four times a week:
Sunday school, followed by morning and afternoon services,
Wednesday-night prayer meetings, and choir rehearsal every
Friday. Fifth Sundays were for communion, testifying and
baptizing. Unlike my mother, her elder sister dressed modestly,
never touched a drop of alcohol and could cut a rug down to
the padding. She never uttered an expletive.

For her part, my aunt was a marvelously plump woman
who was shaped like a hedgehog and stashed money in her
bosom. She cinched her hefty flesh with the triple-bolted
girdle and, with the record player needle dropped on the
right song, Mama's Bible-thumping sister would swing and
swag the Lindy Hop. My mother eschewed such displays of
piety, weighed all of a hundred pounds on a full stomach,
and couldn't dance.

Most of the sweet footing went on in the formal living
room next to the floor model, midcentury Zenith color television. Situated behind pocket doors and a grand entryway
trimmed in ornate crown molding, the room also had wall-to-
wall plush red carpeting, yellow-and-white embroidered sofas
encased in custom plastic slipcovers and decorative mirrors
on the textured damask wallpaper. The room was off-limits,
except on holidays and sometimes Sunday if good company
came over for supper. The whole thing smelled like Scott's
Liquid Gold furniture wax and Woolite rug cleaner.

Auntie Gerald, who integrated the staff at Norwoods
Country Club on Lucas and Hunt Road in north St. Louis
County, did the family shopping at Grandpa Pidgeon's and

a Venture store up on Collinsville Road, and sometimes at Famous-Barr in the sprawling mall over in Belleville. She called it "going up the highway." She loved a Kmart blue-light special almost as much as she enjoyed cornbread soaked in buttermilk. She bought her groceries in bulk, including the box loads of chicken wings and hotdogs that she kept in a deep freezer alongside loaves of Wonder Bread. Every so often, we drove out to a farm beyond Cahokia Mounds to pick turnips, collards, and pole beans.

Uncle Ross lugged in the groceries, saw after the dogs and the yard and burned the garbage in a fire pit when the city went bankrupt and stopped door-to-door trash collection, while my aunt wrung out the laundry and pinned our unmentionables on a clothesline out back. Uncle Ross didn't believe in store-bought dog food or letting his mutts in the house. When the old hounds died, as they commonly did after diets of table scraps and spoiled meat, he buried them in plots around the back garage.

On a block possessed with rooming houses, prostitutes, and drug addicts, we seemed to be better off than most others, except the Sanders siblings—a white judge, lawyer, and librarian—and the friendly loan shark who lived across the street. After we might get caught up in whatever was going on out in the street, Auntie was a strict disciplinarian. Running in the house was forbidden, as were a lot of things, and getting caught either meant a tongue lashing or the business end of Uncle Ross's strap. Which one depended on whether Auntie Gerald was around, in which case the punishment would always be more severe.

"A hard head makes for a soft behind," she'd often say.

When she was feeling good, Auntie would laugh like a schoolgirl, an uncontrolled burst of glee that made her belly jiggle like a bowl of gelatin.

But, that summer, something in Auntie Gerald had changed. She seemed to be angry about everything and at everybody. She had a mean streak that ran as long and deep as the Mississippi. And, for the first time in my life, I was scared of her. The mere sound of my name coming out of her mouth was terrifying.

Every night, as the adults took to their rooms, me and a band of cousins gathered sheets from a closet and slept on the living room floor. Linens were on a first-come-first-serve basis and pillows were in short supply. Most nights, I was left with nothing. So, I started stashing my pallet in Grandma Alice's closet hours before bedtime. I woke up that next morning soaked in blood and urine. Shame washed over me. I was afraid my cousins would see the bloody clothes and laugh at me. So, I sneaked upstairs, washed myself up, stuffed the wet sheets in a trash bag and tucked them into Grandma Alice's closet. Later that day, I heard her calling me from top of the stairs.

"Goldie Taylor! Get your behind on up here!"

I was shaking when I entered her room. She was sitting on the edge of the bed. Bug was in there too, her arms folded and smirking.

"Let me tell you one thang," Auntie Gerald said, jamming her fat finger at me. "You gone quit pissing on my floor!"

"I didn't mean to."

"Your mama didn't say nothing about you pissing on your-self. You dern near thirteen years old. Piss on my carpet again and I'm gone bust your behind, you hear me?"

I nodded my head.

"Say, yes ma'am," my cousin chided.

"Yes, ma'am," I muttered.

"Pissy Annie," Bug said. "That's what we gone call you."

"That's not my name."

"What'chu say, Pissy Annie? You sound like one of them hunkies out in St. Ann."

"So what? That's not my name."

She dived at me, grabbing my neck with both hands. I felt my head hit the floorboards. I couldn't breathe.

"Janice! Jannie-Bug, let that child go!" Grandma Alice screamed. "I said let her go!"

Bug kept choking me, tightening her grip, repeatedly bang-ing my head against the wood slats until I blacked out. I vaguely remember somebody carrying me. I woke up that night in Grandma Alice's bed. The house was silent. I got up and tiptoed downstairs.

Alone in the darkened kitchen pantry, among the stacked canned goods, the canisters of sugar, flour, and dehydrated milk, I braced the telephone on my shoulder. I knew the col-lect long-distance call would register on the next bill from Southwestern Bell, revealing the time and duration. Making long-distance calls, whether to St. Louis County or down to Florida, was strictly forbidden. It would mean another flog-ging and more chores. But, right then, I didn't care about get-ting another whipping. I just wanted to go back to St. Ann. I was desperate to sleep in my own bed again, even if it meant being alone most of the time. While I still harbored a rash of resentment for Mama, I felt like an orphan and didn't want to wake up to somebody else's mother. The operator announced my name and connected the lines.

"Mama, please come get me," I whispered.

"Do you know what time it is? What's wrong with you?"

I heard the creaking floorboards. Somebody was coming up the basement stairs. The noise grew louder. I could hear their feet padding across the dining room now, just on the other side of the wall.

"Mama, please," I said. "Please come get me."

The line went dead. The first blow to my temple, a closed fist, knocked me into the shelving. I remember how it stung, then the numbness and sound of my screams filling my ears.

"Who was you talkin' to?" Bug demanded to know.

I could feel myself trembling. Trapped in the small alcove, I braced myself against the shelving. "Nobody," I mumbled.

I could taste my own blood, the salty tears.

"Who was you talkin' to?"

"Nobody."

Bug grabbed the receiver and reared back as if to swing it. I flinched. She laughed.

"Get-cho stupid ass out that closet."

I stayed awake in the kitchen that night. Afraid to go to sleep, I didn't crawl into my pallet until sometime near dawn.

8

I fell into myself.

Whatever measure of joy I used to find in that house was now eclipsed by terror and mourning. It was a yearning, I suppose, for something that never really had been. There were some experiences, whether with the Farrells or my grandparents, that I had reshaped and romanticized. But, at least in them, I saw a reflection of my own value, of something good. I had been worth something to somebody.

Theirs was a world without bickering or apparent lack. In St. Ann, there were no pugilistic, foul-mouthed cousins, burned-out houses or dead bodies in the alley. Debbie Farrell didn't have to race to the kitchen at dinnertime or fight over the last of anything.

It was then, at twelve, that I marked what I believed was a straight line between morality and wealth. People were poor, I believed, because they were either too dumb or lazy to be anything else. Bug didn't have any better because she didn't want any better, I reasoned. No one disabused me of that notion, not even Grandma Alice.

"Poor folk got poor ways," she would often say.

It was a refrain frequently repeated by my mother and aunts and near about everybody else in our family. It would take me decades to grasp the absurdity in that. However, if I was confused about the functions of poverty and class and what that meant for us, the subjugation of children went without question. By then, there were many other children in the house, including Booky and Uncle Ross's three grandchildren. Our every move was dictated by my aunt, who demanded absolute subservience.

"Honor thy mother and thy father," Auntie Gerald said, misquoting Exodus. "Or your days on this Earth will be short."

That meant that letting the screen door slam, ending a sentence with anything other than "ma'am" or "sir," or failing to sufficiently mollify her petty annoyances could result in a blistered behind, house restriction, or getting locked outside, for sometimes hours at a time, in the hundred-degree heat. Which one depended on how bad we got on her nerves that day. Bible verses were routinely bastardized, if not weaponized, to maintain the hierarchy. All the while, certain pathological behaviors were met with ambivalence and, sometimes, defended or rewarded. In our house, God was something to be feared and, to hear Auntie Gerald tell it, He was still in the smiting business.

If I felt small, it was because I was afforded no significance other than the fact that I was somebody else's child. There were moments when I was treated with outright disdain, like something that could or should be thrown away. I slept fitfully in those first weeks, nursing the pangs of abandonment and betrayal, repeatedly soiling myself in the night.

It was decided then that I couldn't have water after six o'clock. And I had to scrub my sheets and blankets by hand. Figuring I might get tired of the humiliation of getting teased and taunted, Auntie Gerald had me haul the basket out to the open backyard and pin the wet linens to the clothesline in plain view of the neighborhood kids. I thought something was wrong with me, but I was too embarrassed to say anything. When Auntie Killer suggested I might need to see a doctor for bladder problems, Auntie Gerald said I needed my butt busted.

"Ain't nothing wrong with her," Auntie Gerald huffed. "She's just lazy."

Now, as my thirteenth birthday approached, Mama had all but disappeared. I wanted a cake, a party and presents like the Farrell kids got. I wanted to somebody to sing "Happy Birthday" before I blew out my candles. There would be none of that, I knew. I remember crying angry tears.

Bug told anyone who would listen, including Darnell, that I had been "dropped like a bad habit." On top of Pissy Annie and every other ugly name she could think of, she regularly called me "fast." According to her, I was "switching" my hips and chasing behind boys. Since I rarely earned the pleasure of going outside or, even then, beyond our block or the porch swing, there were no boys to chase. Auntie Gerald bought me two training bras and ordered me to stay away from the boys in the neighborhood. That included Darnell, who came around every so often looking for me. But most days I couldn't leave the front steps.

"She cain't come outside," Bug said gleefully. "She on punishment."

That, of course, was cause for more mocking and teasing from my older cousins, especially the boys, who had free rein to come and go as they pleased.

The truth is *fast*, pronounced "fass," is nothing more than a polite synonym for *whore*. It is a calling card, a proverbial welcome mat plastered on a child's reputation that invites public scorn, objectification or, worse, is used to malign and silence victims of molestation and rape. It is tacit approval for the physical sexual exploitation of children. The gentler-sounding "fass" allows the person using it to cloak themselves in innocence while engaging in one of the more despicable forms of body shaming imaginable.

I cannot say for certain if Bug knew what happened to me, but "fass" works to assuage any notion of guilt for the person who commits acts of sexual violence. In other words, the little girl had it coming.

Other cultures have other terms, other cudgels, to describe children who are targeted this way, but "fass" is unique to Black people. And at the time, in our family, I was the only target. I was the little girl who had it coming.

As hard as it was to deal with the near constant mockery, I just wanted them to stop hitting me. I remember praying a lot, then. With nowhere else to turn, I placed a collect call to Grandma Catherine in Florida, who said she would have a talk with my mother.

"If I can't come stay with you, I just want to go home."

"How long has it been?"

"I've been staying here pretty much since school let out."

"Where's your mother?"

"I don't know."

"What do you mean you don't know?"

"She left me."

I'd called collect, but the record of the call still appeared on the monthly statement. When the 305 area code came up on the phone bill, I braced myself. Summertime was always a bad time to get a whipping, if only because wearing shorts left your legs and arms bare to the thrashing. Even so, I wasn't prepared for what came next.

Auntie called me into the bathroom where she was getting dressed. In addition to the itemized, long-distance phone bill, she had heard about the call to my grandmother from Mama.

"If Cat wanted you, you'd be down there with her," she said, squeezing herself into a girdle. "She ain't no dern better than nobody else. Whatever she got, she got it from cleaning them white folk houses. She needs to get that stick out her behind. Somebody gave her two nickels for a dime, and she think she rich."

Auntie Gerald never laid a hand on me. She didn't have to. Her words stung harder than any switch from the yard.

"Bug said my mother isn't coming back."

"Mary Alice'll talk to you about that when she get good and dern ready."

"I want to go home."

"You at home," she sneered. "Stay off my dern phone."

"Yes, ma'am."

"You ain't gone run these streets like you did out there in St. Ann. You a child and you gone stay in a child's place."

"I don't know what you want me to do," I said, sobbing.

"Stop that crying, Goldie Taylor! Ain't nobody gone baby you."

"I don't know what you want me to do," I kept saying, again and again.

She reminded me that, based on scripture, the consequences for disobedience would be an early death. I understood then that there would be no refuge, not in that house or anywhere else. Red-faced and trembling, with snot dripping from my nose, I dared not move until she said so.

"Now get yourself on downstairs."

I sneaked into the kitchen that night, scribbled her name on a slip of yellow notepaper, like Auntie Killer used to do, pissed in a plastic bag, and put it in the bottom of the deep freezer between boxes of frozen chicken wings and hotdogs, and a rack of ribs.

9

The lawn mower was going outside and there was a familiar clanging sound coming from the kitchen. Somebody was running the vacuum cleaner upstairs. The house was being readied for the Fourth of July holiday weekend. Most of the children were still asleep when Auntie Gerald came stomping across the red carpeting.

"Get on up off that floor!" she yelled. "Put some clothes on and make it on in that kitchen."

There were walls to scrub and baseboards to be washed down. We climbed a stepladder to clean the grease off Auntie Gerald's plastic lobsters that hung on the kitchen wall above the stove and swept down the front sidewalk with bleach water. Uncle Ross cut the front and side lawns and hoisted an American flag on the freshly painted porch column.

We weren't celebrating the birth of a country or even the men and women in our family who had served in the military. Just as Thanksgiving was never a remembrance of Pilgrims, the Fourth, for us, was more like a family reunion. Soon, the house would be burgeoning with cousins and in-laws and other folk we didn't see but two or three times a year. They would come to laugh and jostle and fill their bellies with beer and Vess sodas and food, and then fall out on the sofas and chairs to sleep it off. For the most part, unless a liquor-infused fistfight broke out over the card table, the holidays still hold some of my fondest memories. Mama would come too, I knew. She'd be dressed up, wearing her good lipstick, a bouffant wig and fake eyelashes. She'd laugh over beers with Auntie Killer and fix herself a plate of ribs and mustard-potato salad. Invariably, somebody would say how much we looked alike.

I'd get to see Auntie Killer and Uncle Willie, who would come with pans of baked beans and macaroni salad nobody dared to eat. Auntie Gerald hadn't forgotten about what she'd done with that ziplock bag full of urine. Ironically and unbeknownst to her, her own name was presently suspended in a frozen pool of piss.

Booky and I helped Uncle Ross scrape the grill and get a first crack at the bag of fireworks. When Auntie wasn't looking, he'd always slip us a few rounds of Black Cat bottle rockets and a sleeve of matches he knew we weren't supposed to have. Booky usually managed to come up with a cache of forbidden Roman candles to shoot off in the alley. Boys from around the block were already lighting up their stash, but Uncle Ross said we had to get our work done before he cut us loose.

Me and Booky got busy out back clearing weeds and dead brush. After an hour in the hot sun, my legs grew unsteady, and my knees buckled.

"You light-headed, Red?" my uncle called over.

"Yes, sir."

Uncle Ross sent me inside to get some water and sit for a while under a window-mounted air-conditioning. Aunt Gerald was fussing over a lemon meringue pie when I walked in the back door. Booky came huffing in behind me.

"Ge'challs behinds on back outdoors!"

Just then, Booky, sick from the heat, threw up. Dizzy, red-faced and sweating profusely, I could barely hold myself upright.

I tried to explain why we were sent inside. Auntie Gerald was immediately suspicious. She berated us for playing sick. Grandma Alice filled two Styrofoam cups with water from the kitchen sink. Booky took a swig and immediately threw up on the linoleum floor. Auntie Gerald sent me into the basement to get some towels to mop up the vomit.

Downstairs, on the backside of the basement, I stumbled onto a cardboard box filled with things that had been stolen from my mama's house in St. Ann a few months earlier, including the headphones and tape recorder my grandparents had given me for Christmas. Neither of which would've been worth a trip to a pawnshop. I kept looking, hoping to find the blue-boxed record player Mama gave me. I didn't find it, though it was immediately clear to me who the culprit was. It was not the first time Auntie Gerald's oldest son broke into our house nor would it be the last.

Ronnie Lee was always in some sort of a bind, legal or otherwise. I don't remember him ever having a job and I don't know how far along he got in school. But, after a stint in an Illinois state penitentiary, he ran the streets morning, noon, and night. Ronnie Lee limped into the house at various hours, generally to get something to eat or nap in the basement. By my count, he had at least nine children by then. He'd been shot in the ass once, though he never could say straight on who did it or why anybody would want to spray him with buckshot. I always figured it was either because he stole something or didn't pay somebody back.

Ronnie Lee was a prolific thief. In '68, our upstairs neighbor on Interdrive spotted him loading Mama's fur coat and our television set onto a moving truck. When my father found out, he tracked my cousin down, snatched him by the collar, and repeatedly drove his fist into Ronnie Lee's face until his knuckles were bloody. When he was through punching his lights out, Daddy took him to the emergency room and paid cash to have his jaw wired. My father had just beaten a manslaughter charge the prior year for stomping a Korean exchange student to death outside my godmother's tavern. But Daddy was dead now, and Ronnie Lee was still a crook. Rummaging through the box, I fished out one of the cassette tapes Grandpa Roy had given me. I put the broken earphones and the recorder in a gap that ran along the stairs that separated the stacked stone foundation from the basement. Auntie Gerald used to store Mason jars of fruit and vegetables in the dusty alcove. But farther up, near the stop step, Uncle Ross kept his stash of *Hustler* magazines tucked between folds of newspapers. I figured it was as safe of a place as any.

Later that afternoon, I was polishing the stairway banister when I heard the floorboards shifting over my head. A creaking noise was coming from upstairs. At first, I thought it might be our great-aunt Josie, whose ghost was known to haunt the upper hallway. I wanted to get a good look at her, so I eased up the stairs, inching along on my stomach over the red carpeting, until I got to the quarter landing. I could see Ronnie Lee in Grandma Alice's room. He was rifling through her things. She'd taken her pocketbook with her when she left to go to choir rehearsal with Auntie Gerald, but her tithing envelope was tucked inside her Bible on the nightstand. He shook the pages until it came tumbling out. I slid back down the stairs and ducked into the kitchen, where I pretended to be reading. I heard the front door slam on his way out.

Scarcely a week went by when somebody didn't steal something from somebody and that somebody was almost always Ronnie Lee. Uncle Ross bought a padlock for Grandma Alice's bedroom door, and she kept the key pinned inside her bra. That didn't stop the thief from unscrewing the metal hasp from the side doorjamb to break in. Grandma Alice was forced to start locking her checkbook and cash in a metal chifforobe.

That day, when she discovered her money was gone, her wailing filled the house. I didn't like seeing her like that, so I broke down and said it was Ronnie Lee. I told Uncle Ross about the headphones and the tape recorder I found in the basement, too. As proof, I showed him the John Coltrane cassette.

"I saw him up in her room."

Grandma Alice broke down crying again, but Auntie Gerald blamed me for starting trouble.

"How we know you ain't bring that mess with you?" Auntie Gerald said. "You can't put that on Ronnie. We don't know how that got down there."

She was as mad as I'd ever seen her. Ronnie Lee was furious. He denied ever breaking into Mama's house and said he never touched Grandma Alice's money.

"You stole Grandma Alice's money! And I saw you!" I shouted. "Wait until my mama finds out that you're the one who broke in our house!"

When he yanked an extension cord from an electric fan and wrapped one end around his knuckles, I jetted from the house just as my mother was pulling into the gravel driveway. I didn't recognize her car. Mama was driving a new burgundy two-door Pontiac Sunbird.

I was all at once relieved to see her and terrified that she might think, as usual, that I had done something to upset the apple cart. The only thing that I could really count on was that nobody would hit me when she was looking.

Uncle Ross met her on the gray patio stone walkway that ran between the front steps and the driveway. Out there in front of the rosebushes, he explained what was happening.

She stared at the grass as Uncle Ross talked.

I had been living there for nearly a month by then, routinely getting beat on and harassed by ne'er-do-well cousins, every day more terrible than the last. I had begged Mama to let me come home and, now that she was here, if only to cel-

ebrate the holiday with family, I realized that for her I was
the problem. Mama shot me an angry glance.

It had been weeks since I last saw her, but if I thought for
a moment that she would come to my rescue, I was wrong.
Ronnie Lee denied chasing after me with the gray electri-
cal cord and, again, this time tearfully, he denied burglariz-
ing our house.

"Auntie Mary Alice, you know I wouldn't never take nothing from you."

Mama knew better than that, but let it pass.

The look on her face said she didn't believe him. She wasn't
exactly taking his side, but she was mad that I had caused the
commotion.

"You gone learn to be quiet, child," she said. "But I can't
have you whipping on her, Ronnie Lee."

"I ain't do nothing," he said. "I swear on Mama's grave."

"Yes, you did!" I shouted.

"I said keep your mouth shut," Mama said.

There were at least three adults who saw Ronnie Lee
threaten me and none of them said a word.

"You ain't gotta lie on my brother like that!" Bug said. "He
ain't done nothing to you!"

"He broke in our house and stole our stuff. I know that
much," I said. "I found my Christmas presents down in the
basement."

"You a lie!" Bug shot back.

"You wouldn't know the truth if it bit you in the ass!" I
yelled.

Any other time, Bug might've snatched me up by the throat
and choked me out. But my mother was standing there.

"Shut your damn mouth, Goldie Taylor!" Mama said, clapping her hands to punctuate the syllables.

"She's always talking crazy and punching on me."

Mama turned to Bug and asked, "Is that true?"

"Ain't touched that little girl," Bug said.

"Liar! Even Auntie Gerald know you lying. Go ahead, call me dumb and retarded like you always do."

"Ain't nobody called you no damn retarded," Bug said with a huff.

"That's what's wrong with her now, Mary Alice," Auntie Gerald said. "She'ont know when to shut up. You done told her ninety-nine times and she still talking. She too grown for me."

I suspect my mother knew I was telling the truth, though she wouldn't say one way or the other. That didn't sit well with her sister.

"If she'ont wanna live by my rules, you need to carry her on out of here with you, Mary Alice."

I felt betrayed. Not just by my mother, but everybody living in that house. Not even Grandma Alice spoke up. I went to her room and stayed there well into the evening. At some point, tempers cooled, and the house filled up with extended family. The rest of Ronnie Lee's children arrived, and I could hear the revelry going on downstairs. Along with the rest of the kids, they piled into the family Buick to see the fireworks on the Mississippi.

"Golleh," Grandma Alice said, in her Mississippi drawl, "y'ont wanna go wit'em?"

"No, ma'am. I can see it from here."

The riverfront fireworks were still booming in the sky

and blossoming over the horizon when my mother's boy-friend arrived. The family liked L.C. almost as much as they liked seeing my mother with him. He stayed a while, toss-ing back beers with her in the kitchen. I liked seeing her in love, even if he didn't seem to care much about me. By the time I worked up the nerve to go downstairs, Mama already had her purse slung over her shoulder. I didn't get any far-ther than the stair landing before I chickened out and turned back. A short while later, from my grandmother's side win-dow, I watched them get into their cars and follow one an-other onto the street.

Grandma pulled off her clothes and got dressed for bed.

"Here, child, put this on," she said, handing me one of her long nightgowns.

We crawled under the covers together. I snuggled up to her bosom and closed my eyes.

"Never go to sleep mad, child," Grandma Alice said. "If you look at anything long enough, good, bad or the other, you can see God in it."

"Grandmamma, why did Jesus take my mama from me?"

10

L.C. was the first man who hadn't beat on my mother and she loved him endlessly. My father may have plied her with platinum bouffant wigs and taffeta pantsuits and taken her to high-end galas, but L.C. gave her the kind of stability she'd longed for her entire life. He enjoyed her home cooking, though it wasn't exactly her forte, and Mama dutifully fixed his plates. Despite the fact he was bedding other women, both known and unknown to her, she treated him like he was her personal king. One lady lived on the next block, but L.C. wasn't shy about letting his car be seen outside Auntie Gerald's house every holiday.

He was a love like none she had ever known, and I knew marriage was never far from her mind. L.C. didn't reek of cheap liquor. He was physically a strong man with a serious countenance, who wasn't ashamed to bellow with laughter in mixed company. L.C. wasn't particularly studied, and I doubt he earned a college degree, but he had something the others did not. There was an unmistakable sense of maturity and order about him.

All that summer, I fantasized about what I thought would be normal life—a home with a mother and father like the Farrells had. I wanted Mama to marry L.C. and take me back. He never said a harsh word to me, but he let it be known that he wasn't particularly interested in stepping into shoes that weren't his to fill. And I knew, even then, that there wasn't anything Mama wouldn't do for him and nothing she would not give up. Even if that something was me.

One Saturday morning, Mama called to say she was coming to take me school clothes shopping at JCPenney. Uncle Ross told her I needed new shoes and underwear. With puberty now in full stride, by late August, I'd grown out of most everything I came with. I got dressed and waited.

She didn't get there until near on nine o'clock that night. The mall was closing by then. I was sitting on the front porch steps, whining like a hound, when she pulled up. She didn't explain why, but her car was packed with her dresses still on their hangers and taped-up boxes. She stayed long enough to hand over the last of my books and few things from my old room. After a hushed conversation, Mama wrote Auntie a check to take me shopping and left. Uncle Ross said she was moving in with L.C. My heart broke into a million pieces.

I was tired of watching her come and go and, at that moment, I didn't care if she ever came back. I hated her for taking up L.C. and giving up our house. I hated her for leaving me.

The following weekend, Mama showed up unannounced

and took me with her to L.C.'s two-bedroom townhouse out
I-64 in O'Fallon. It was brand-new. Bits of construction dust
still covered the ground and the concrete walkways were still
drying out. At some point that night, Mama turned off the
television and went to load the dishwasher.

"Where's Lucky?"

"I left her with Miss Fran. She'll take good care of her.
L.C. is allergic to cats."

"Is he allergic to kids too?"

"Watch yourself."

"Am I moving in with you?"

"We'll talk about that later," she said. "Head on upstairs,
take a bath and get to bed. It's late."

"Mama?"

"You heard me. I said later."

L.C. came in from work sometime after midnight. Awak-
ened by the sounds of their lovemaking in the next room, I
slept fitfully.

The drive back to East St. Louis the next morning was
eerily quiet. My mother, who stood just under five feet tall,
was always too short to see over the dashboard of her car, so
she sat on a pillow with the bucket seat launched all the way
to the front. I remember how tiny she looked that morning,
gripping the steering wheel with both hands, as she always
did, and staring at the roadway. Paul Harvey was on the radio
delivering his segment, *The Rest of the Story*, as we tooled
along the highway. She lit a cigarette, took a drag, and flicked
the butts in the ashtray. There was no sound other than the
whoosh of winds that flowed through the open windows.

When Mama dropped me off at Auntie Gerald's that morning, I thought it might be the last time I'd see her. I opened
the passenger-side door, stepped out onto the street, and
walked into the house, saying nothing.

I had always assumed I would be going home at some
point, though that seemed unlikely now. A full year after I
was raped, after I kept swallowing pills until I gagged and
choked them into a toilet, I was starting to let go of her or
at least any delusion I had about what I thought life was supposed to look like. I hunched my shoulders as she drove away.

"What you sad for?" Auntie Gerald said, getting dressed
for church. "Ain't no sense in you pouting. You got a place
to stay and a roof over your head."

"I'm not sad," I said. "Just disappointed."

Auntie Gerald shrugged and scoffed.

"You ain't lived long enough to know what that mean.
You gone be disappointed a lot in this life, you know that?"

"Yes, ma'am, but it don't make it feel no better now."

"Let your mama get herself together. She'll be back for
you."

"I don't want her to come back."

"You don't mean that."

"She don't want me and I don't want her either."

"Honor thy mother and thy father," Auntie Gerald said.

"They supposed to take care of they kids."

At Auntie Gerald's house, I stammered and stuttered, too
afraid of saying something that might upset my aunt or draw
the ire of my older cousins. Speaking out of turn, about
grown-folk business, in church, at the dinner table when

your mouth was full, and at almost any other point in the day, anything other than a "yes, ma'am" or a "yes, sir" could spell real trouble. There were times, though, fleeting moments like these, when Auntie Gerald saw the world as I did: replete with disappointments about what we thought we deserved, how we wanted to be treated, when we had decisions to make about what we were willing to live without. More frequently, though, Auntie Gerald reminded us that children were to be seen and not heard. The consequences for disobedience were clearly spelled out in the Bible, she said.

"Honor thy mother and thy father, or thy days will be short."

Coming up, I believed every word of that, whether it meant getting a beating that made you wish you were dead or a bolt of lightning sailing out of the sky. It was, I would learn, a weaponized version of Exodus 20:12, which reads: "Honor thy father and thy mother: that thy days may be long upon the land which the Lord thy God giveth thee."

Still, she was capable of boundless compassion. She knew I was hurting and, I'm sure, she knew why. She also knew that I longed to be with my mother, even when it seemed there was no room for me in her life. In her own way, Auntie Gerald tried to fill the gap. She knew it might never be enough.

The spots of kindness never lasted long. I knew to keep quiet, especially when she was watching *The Young and the Restless* and *As the World Turns*. Even so, I sometimes pissed myself at the sound of my own name and my lips quivered when Auntie Gerald called me Dum-Dum.

"You got all the book smarts in the world, Dum-Dum,

but you know one thing? You ain't got a dern lick of common sense," Auntie regularly chided.

I'm not stupid! I screamed out in my head.

But nothing she ever did or said was worse than the day I heard her telling somebody that I was sexually active and that she wouldn't be surprised if I turned up pregnant.

I was sweeping down the carpeted stairs that afternoon, doing my best to stay invisible when I spotted her sitting in the living room in her big chair. The phone receiver was braced against her shoulder as she folded a hamper of clothes wedged between her legs. I didn't know who she was talking to, but she told them I was fass. I froze. I felt a quake in my chest and swallowed my tears. It was then that I knew what they knew; that something had happened to me and, for that, I was to blame. She either wanted me to hear her or didn't care if I had.

"She over here because Mary Alice can't keep up with her," she said, glancing up at me.

Auntie kept me on a tight leash and now I knew why. The reason I couldn't leave the block and was often ordered to stay in the house had less to do with the dangers outside than who she thought I was. I assumed then that all the women in the family believed it and thought me a whore. After all, there was little or nothing my mother, aunts and grandmother did not talk about. I thought God, the vengeful one Auntie Gerald so often warned me about, was paying me back for throwing toilet paper in the neighbor's trees.

"Yes, yes, shol'nuf," she told the caller.

11

More and more, Grandma Alice became my safe harbor. And, in some ways, I was hers. I watched over her room when she wasn't around. And I made sure she got her black coffee and tucked away two eggs in the back of the crisper, so she could hard boil them for breakfast in the morning. When family fistfights, pissing matches, and my aunt's brutish nature took their toll, I clung to my grandmother's hip.

We listened to the Cardinals play baseball up in her room. As Jack Buck's play-by-play on AM-KMOX crackled from the transistor, I could see the glowing crown of stadium lights hovering in the sky from her window. I often fell asleep in her bed with my head in her breasts.

If she smelled trouble brewing, Grandma Alice sometimes intervened with a "go on 'way from here" or "let that chile 'lone." She couldn't always spare me from the emotional upheaval or the physical attacks, nor did she always try. Even so, my aunt went easier on me when Grandma Alice was around.

In 1963, before I was a twinkle in anybody's eye, Grandma Alice worked in the Continental Trailways bus depot on Seventh and Broadway at the terminal restaurant. Her job entailed cutting cakes and pies. The café, with its daisy-colored vinyl bar stools, high-backed booths and Formica counters, was segregated, as was everything else in that era. Mama remembers her bringing home slices of lemon pound cake and apple pie.

While it's not clear when she started, it is the only job anybody can remember my grandmother having, outside of "keeping house" for white people down in Osceola. When she turned sixty-five in 1966, Mama and Auntie Gerald told her she didn't have to pull any more shifts in the bus depot.

The promise of better-paying jobs and at least a meager portion of liberty are what drew my grandparents north, first to Arkansas from Mississippi and then on to Missouri. They arrived in mid-1933, the year after Auntie Gerald was born. Grandpa Joe got a job chasing hogs and working a barge on the river.

In her mind, there were two kinds of people in the world, the stupid and the blessed. Auntie Gerald said I was some of both, but my insatiable reading habits were seen as something of an anathema in our family.

"She can take to anything you put down in front of her," Grandma Alice used to tell folks.

"She smart as a whip, but ain't got no dern common sense," Auntie Gerald would invariably chime in.

Being able to answer various game show questions that left

Grandma Alice and Auntie Gerald scratching their heads was sometimes met with wonder and delight. Auntie Gerald never had to hunt down a calculator when she had me to run the numbers through my head. Most often, though, it was used as a cudgel to chastise me if she felt embarrassed.

"You still a dum-dum," she'd say.

I was too scared to speak up in my own defense. Doing that would only make things worse, which meant they always got the last word. Grandma Alice, who never once called me anything other than by my given name, said I should love them all the same.

"Y'ont get but one family," she used to tell me. "Shit, love don't always come packed up and pretty like you want it."

I suppose that was her way of putting salve on the open sores. She knew I was hurting, but she wanted me to love as she had, never hesitant or wavering or receding. I could not see my way to that right then, and I doubted I ever would. Though I sometimes longed for it, I had no such grace. I wanted to see and feel the world as she did, one that didn't crush and maim. If she had any dreams, other than for health and peace for her family, she never once spoke of them out loud.

On what had to be Friday, because Grandma Alice was in the kitchen frying fish in a skillet, I wandered in and sat down. I asked about my mother again.

"Grandmamma, is my mama coming back this time?"

"She ain't never leave. Your mama got it hard out there, baby," she told me. "She can't look after you."

"I do okay by myself."

I didn't so much miss my mother as I did miss having one. I couldn't point to the exact moment when she stopped, but at some point—long before she dropped me off at Auntie Gerald's house with nothing more than a few recycled grocery bags worth of clothes—I knew the pieces would never quite fall together again. Grandma Alice, like Auntie Gerald, kept insisting that the situation was temporary, that my mother had some hills to climb, and that it was better not to have me weighing her down.

"Who gone fry you some fish?" she said with a chuckle. "Your mama cain't boil water good."

I smiled as she let the jack fish soak with the tails still on in a pan of ice-cold milk.

"Love'll be right there where you left it," she said.

She then dredged the long, narrow pieces in densely seasoned cornmeal. The fire was up too high again and the grease was smoking.

"You should turn down the stove, Grandmamma."

When she was done, Grandma Alice set out some chopped onions, sliced pickles, mustard, and hot sauce. I pulled the flaky sections of fish off the long spiny bone and made a sandwich with two pieces of Wonder Bread.

"Y'ont want none of this spaghetti?"

Before I could answer, we heard Auntie Gerald stomping on the ceiling. Sometimes she called us that way and it was expected that we would come running.

"Goldie Taylor, where you at?" Auntie Gerald yelled from the top of the stairs.

I scrambled out of the kitchen, through the dining room and to the bottom step.

"Ma'am?"

"I thought I told you to clean this dern bathroom?"

"I was finna do it after I finished helping Grandmamma with the fish."

"You a lie and the truth ain't in you. You ain't doing nothing but stuffing your face. Get on up here at get this ring out this tub and bring that vacuum with you. How am I 'sposed take a bath in this molly tub?"

"Yes, ma'am."

Auntie Gerald was still fussing, and I was getting it for old and new as I dragged the Hoover up the steps.

"Mary Alice done spoiled you," she said, jamming her finger in my face. "Listen here, you can stay up under my mama if you wanna and I'll still bust your tail. You hear me, Goldie Taylor?"

"Yes, ma'am."

I felt my face tuning up. Gripping the vacuum cleaner handle and gritting my teeth, I let the tears run down my cheeks.

"You wanna hit me, little girl?" she said, sneering at me nose-to-nose. "If you do, you better knock me out and get to running."

I said nothing.

"Hush up and dry your face. Ain't nobody touched you yet."

When I was finished cleaning the commode, the sink and every other surface with Soft Scrub, and Auntie Gerald was satisfied at the look of things, she handed me a sponge and a bottle of Murphy's Oil Soap.

"Wipe them banisters down," she said. "And make sure you get between them cornices in the railing."

Between sponging shoe tracks off the linoleum floors and polishing hardwood balustrades, at times suicidal and still engaging in self-harm, I worried that my life would end there in that house.

I was still weeping when Uncle Ross got home and passed me coming up the stairs.

"What'd you go and do now, Red?"

"I didn't do anything. I swear."

When I wasn't doing housework, I'd hide away in Grandma Alice's room to read. I was happy to have my collection of novels and poetry, despite the teasing that ensued. Bug said other than the Sanders family and some of the prostitutes hitting up out-of-state cars over on Collinsville Avenue, the people in my books were the only white people in town. My cousin Michael, who typically called me Dirty Red, jokingly said my new name was "Encyclopedia Brown."

"But he's white," I said.

"That's okay," Michael responded. "You think you white, too. Stay around here long enough and you'll get some Black on you."

As a practice, moving children between family members was not uncommon in Black America and is rooted in African culture. Despite my having lived with her off and on for long stretches of time, my aunt never had legal custody

of me or any of the other children who came to stay in her
house. No matter how long I was there, in the eyes of the
US government, I still lived with my mother, who received
monthly Social Security survivor's benefits in my name after
my father's death. A check, in a recognizable brown envelope,
would arrive on the third of every month until I reached my
eighteenth birthday.

By law, Bug told me, that disbursement followed me. If
I moved to Florida with Grandma Cat, she said my mother
would lose the money. I understood then why I was given
over to my mother's sister rather than shipped off to Miami.
Part of it, I know, also had to do with that check, but also
L.C.'s stated disinterest in children and my mother's long
hours at work. She couldn't see after me, as Grandma Alice
had explained, and now that was compounded by the specter
of my own nascent sexuality. To Auntie Gerald and everyone else who lived there, I was a whore, a smart aleck, and
a hell-raising, wanna-be-white, trouble-starting fantastical
liar who needed to be kept underfoot. Looking back, I saw
myself and the world as clearly as any thirteen-year-old girl
might. I didn't want the life I had, but thought I was unwor-
thy of anything better.

At thirteen, I had become Auntie's personal page and stew-
ard, which meant among other things fetching her food,
washing her dishes, and pinning her oversize brassieres and
drawers on the line. Unlike the other children in the house,
I was expected to remain within earshot during nearly every
waking hour, on the off chance Auntie Gerald wanted a Pepsi
or some hand-packed ice cream from the store. And I was not

allowed to be alone in the company of any boy who wasn't related to us.

It also meant whacking weeds in the lot next door and shoveling garbage into the firepit in the backyard. It meant bleaching down the sidewalk, letting Comet-laced water soak in the tub until the gray scummy ring rubbed off, and scrubbing cakes of oil and spillage off the stove with a dry wool sometimes until my fingers were scaly and bleeding. My days were consumed with scouring pots, mopping floors, sweeping down the stairs and waxing furniture. Almost as soon as I finished one chore, she'd find another.

"An idle mind is the Devil's playground."

Work came before food and sometimes before the sun. And even then, you had to beat the others to the pot before the rations were depleted. We lined up with our single-ply paper plates and washed our meals down with cups of lemonade made from tap water, sugar, and bottles of ReaLemon juice.

Out of desperation, I stole a postage stamp off Auntie's dresser and wrote Grandma Cat a letter. She replied with only a belated birthday card and a ten-dollar bill, which Auntie Gerald took for herself, mumbling something about tithing and claiming I owed church choir dues as she stuffed it into her bosom.

I prayed for God to strike her down.

SOMEBODY HAVE MERCY

12

As the end of summer neared, Auntie Gerald's house was still full of children. Besides my cousins Peety, Fat Man, and Booky, Uncle Ross's daughter Bernadette and three grandchildren were staying there, too. That included an older cousin, a high school basketball player, who I came to loathe. At over six feet, Uncle Ross's fifteen-year-old grandson was almost as tall as he was dumb. He ate like a vulture, smelled like a bubbling sewer, and had the mental capacity of a rusty lug wrench.

There were two granddaughters, an older girl we called Pudgie and one a month younger than me, but behind in school because she'd been "put back." They were cousins by marriage, bound not by blood or water, but an ill-fated crossing of the stars. All three were bug-eyed and the girls were gap-toothed like their mother, who was the spitting image of Uncle Ross.

The good news is none of them were pugilistic brawlers like Bug and some of the others. They'd spent several years in Hawaii, where their father was stationed in the Army, and came sporting matching black bomber jackets emblazoned with colorful Japanese dragons. They were a decidedly goatish bunch, ill-mannered and raucous when their grandmother, my aunt, wasn't around and decidedly sanguine when she was. Though, there was only so long that lid could be kept on the pot.

Prone to histrionics, but otherwise good-natured and waggish, Pudgie claimed to have seen Great-Aunt Josie's apparition in the house one night. She bolted out the front door, as one apparently does when they've seen a ghost, crying, and screaming and tearing off her clothes.

"I saw her! I saw her! I saw Aunt Josie! I saw Aunt Jos-eeeeee!"

Aunt Josie sightings were far from unusual. The reports of otherworldly activity in the house came almost as frequently as Lou Brock stole bases in Busch Stadium. Pudgie, though, was a garden-variety, dim-witted lunatic. She was always the first one to catch the Holy Spirit in church, and I guess if I were a ghost, she'd be the one I'd pick on, if only to watch her whoop and holler and yank her top off in the middle of the street. That kind of delirium, even in a family like ours, was uncommon. Pudgie was a different kind of crazy.

With Auntie Gerald, Uncle Ross, and the rest of the grown folks down the street at the Regal Room for an Elks Lodge dance, we were home alone that night and had the run of the house. Among other things, we got into uncle's stock of

Manischewitz and Mogen David wines, of which we drank copious amounts while playing "Never Have I Ever." There didn't appear to be much of anything the boy hadn't done and, true to form, the youngest girl was slow with the confessionals. Peety holed up in the kitchen, talking to her boyfriend on the telephone well after the hour when such things were forbidden.

Oblivious to the rules of the game, Pudgie kept swigging when it wasn't her turn. By the time the second bottle was finished and her brother had confessed to everything short of a felony, she was claiming she saw a picture frame tip over in the living room. Well, that scared the piss out of everybody, especially a particularly superstitious boy like Booky.

The idea of a ghost in the house had me shaking in my sandals. My mama and Auntie Killer both owned Ouija boards, but I was afraid to touch them. Auntie Gerald warned us about fooling with such things.

"Open that dern door and y'ont know what might come in," she'd say.

When my copy of *Jane Eyre* went missing, Bernadette blamed Auntie Josie. Another, Katherine Porter's *Flowering Judas and Other Stories*, soon met the same fate when I left it on the kitchen table. I'd read *The Jilting of Granny Weatherall* dozens of times, but now the old gal and her fevered rantings had disappeared. The same went for my journals, which I had begun keeping with some regularity after I came back from Miami.

The books weren't the only things to go missing. Sometimes, it was a freshly pressed pleated church skirt or one of the patent leather shoes Auntie Gerald bought me from Kmart.

"Goldie Taylor, you better find that dern shoe," Auntie demanded. "You cain't hop on one foot to church."

Bernadette giggled and said, "Ask Aunt Josie what she did with it."

I was forced to wear sneakers that Sunday and the next, until the shoe turned up behind the radiator in the dining room.

The night Pudgie said she saw Aunt Josie, she bolted from the house and we had to coax her back inside. I decided to sleep with Grandma Alice. It wasn't such a good idea, that being Aunt Josie's old bedroom. The unmistakable smell of lilies wafted in the air, which were Josephine's favorite. Still tipsy from sips of wine, I hid my head under the covers until I heard Uncle Ross stumble through the front door. He quickly fell asleep on his recliner, snoring so hard the vibrations could be felt through the floorboards. I felt better knowing he was downstairs.

Aunt Josie, a diminutive gray-haired spinster, was known to walk the stairs in the middle of the night and sometimes showed up in the dining room before sunrise like she was waiting on somebody to bring her breakfast. Every so often, even in the dead of summer, the house took on a bone-numbing chill. Doors shut themselves, drawers opened on their own, and breezes flowed through the upper hallway for seemingly no reason at all.

"Aunt Josie must be going to the bathroom," Bernadette would say.

★ ★ ★

I missed our life in St. Ann. I wanted to go home, but right then, I didn't know exactly where that was. The full summer had gone by and I hadn't once seen my sister, who was now married and living with her baby in her mother-in-law's basement. My brother, Donnie, was now staying with a girl named Wilma in a two-room apartment up on Pennsylvania Avenue around the corner from Auntie Gerald's house. He ping-ponged between Wilma and Beverly, and they frequently came to blows over my brother's fleeting affections. Unable to hold down a job bussing tables in a restaurant for more than a few months at a time, Donnie lived mostly off a general assistance check and food stamps. He could barely keep up the rent at the flophouse without loans from Mr. Rent Man.

By then, Mama had given up on the idea that he would finish high school and pick up a meaningful trade. When Donnie wasn't hosting impromptu pot parties or snuggled up with his latest squeeze on his waterbed, he'd come around Auntie Gerald's house for a hot plate. My mother was largely ambivalent about his comings and goings.

As for me, I was caught up with Jane Austen's series of novels. A county library desk clerk back in St. Ann, with whom I'd worn out my welcome, had pointed me to the aisle. I started imagining what it was like to be Elizabeth Bennett, the second-oldest sister in *Pride and Prejudice*. She was pretty and confident and wanted. By the time I finished the novel, I was dead set on finding my mother a good husband. I figured we should try a marriage market.

I remember the day I barged into the bathroom and sat on

the edge of the tub. My mother was slipping on her panty-hose for work when I came up with a big idea.

"Mama, can we go to a ball?"

"What're you going on about now?"

"That's where ladies go to find a husband," I said. "We could get dressed up and go get one for you. Maybe there's one like Mr. Farrell."

"You done lost your mind."

"That's how they do it in this book I'm reading."

"And what book is that?"

"Pride and Prejudice."

"Go outside and play."

The Austen novels were in the bags Mama brought over to Auntie Gerald's and I hadn't been back to turn them in. Now that she was living with L.C., I rarely saw her. When I did, she always seemed to be in a hurry to get somewhere else.

I was writing then. I kept rambling short stories and poems in a stack of spiral-bound notebooks stuffed in a shoebox under Grandma Alice's bed. Like the English novels I collected and rarely returned on time to the public library, out of shame, I hid them. After all, I had been raised by women who dropped their stillborn babies in a cotton field and men who lied about their ages to go to war for the benefit of a monthly stipend. When I was of age, I would be expected to get a marginally decent job, punch a clock, get married and make sure my children got clothed and fed. I would not be expected to write poems or anything else somebody might see fit to print.

Writers, a librarian once told me, were destitute drunk-

ards or, worse, clinically insane like Edgar Allan Poe and
Ernest Hemingway. My family was littered with those sorts
of people—drug addicts and alcoholics, single welfare moth-
ers living in cold-water flats, and those with a cacophony of
mental health issues—and I wanted no part of it.

Sometime in mid-August, a few weeks before the opening
of a new school year, Auntie Gerald was in the kitchen frying a pan of chicken wings.

"Hand me that paprika out the cabinet," she said.

"Yes, ma'am."

As she sprinkled heavy doses of garlic and onion powder
in a bowl of flour, she said, "I talked to your mama and I'm
going to put you in school over here."

I wanted to be angry but, right then, I felt nothing. She
never looked up.

Come Labor Day, the house filled up with family again.
After we stuffed our bellies with ribs, potato salad and collard
greens, Donnie asked to borrow Mama's car. She might've
thought better of it, but she was three beers in and swaying
on her feet. My brother promised he was going straight to the
store and coming right back. The quick errand turned into
an hours-long drug binge.

Mama was stone sober and pacing the living floor when
we heard tires skid down the street. The first boom set off a
panic in the house. A second boom shook the house. Uncle
Ross rushed out the front door. A speeding car had hit a curb
and flipped. The roof hit the pavement. The roadway was littered with glass and metal.

Mama recognized her car and took off in full stride. I heard her screaming, "Donnie! Donnie!"

Her knees buckled beneath her. She dropped to her knees, planted her palms on the concrete walkway, and started praying out loud.

Shouts and cries seemed to be coming from everywhere. Auntie Gerald wrapped herself around me and led me back up on the porch. I broke free.

"Let her go, Geraldine," somebody said.

I ran up the sidewalk, calling out his name. I could see him twisted upside down, still in the driver's seat.

"Donnie! Donnie!" I shouted. "Donnie!"

He wedged himself free and crawled from the wreckage. His face was covered in blood. Unable to hold himself up, he closed his eyes and fell in the middle of the road. Somebody stopped the oncoming traffic. Uncle Ross rushed out to get him. A woman I didn't recognize spread a blanket on the ground.

"Lay down here, son," she said. "Help is coming."

His eyes were closed. His mouth hung open.

"No!" I scream. "Please don't die!"

Fire trucks rolled down the block, followed by an ambulance. The medics turned him over and started working on him. One of them said, "He got a hold of something bad."

He started convulsing.

"Lord Jesus, have mercy," Grandma Alice cried. "Have mercy on him, Father."

There had been other binges, other transgressions, including an arrest after another wreck that required a sizable cash bond. Sometimes Mama put him out, sometimes he left on his own, but there was never a point when she stopped trying to save his life. Once, Mama was forced to pawn her wedding rings my father gave her at a shop over on Easton Avenue to get him out. She lost her jewelry, she later lamented, when she couldn't keep up the payments.

That night, Donnie was stabilized, placed in a neck brace, strapped to a board, and loaded onto a stretcher. He was awake and breathing. Tears rolled down his temples.

"I'm sorry, Jo," he said, calling Mama by her nickname.

13

I unraveled rows of pink sponge curlers, fluffed out my hair and spritzed on Afro Sheen oil spray. The clothes weren't anything as nice as Grandma Cat bought, but they were new, purchased at a Venture store up in Collinsville. Auntie Gerald promised to take me to Sears when she had time. I tried smudging on some of Bug's makeup that morning to camouflage the sprinkling of pimples that dotted my forehead. The Fashion Fair foundation was far too dark for my complexion. Between that and the Maybelline black eyeliner I used to thicken my brows, I looked more a midpubescent Rocky Raccoon than Brooke Shields.

Auntie Gerald poked her head in the bathroom and said, "Wash that mess off your face and let's go."

She waited outside in the car with the motor running, while I finished getting ready.

"You shave up under your arms and put deodorant on?" she asked as I got in shotgun.

"Yes, ma'am."

When she was satisfied that I was presentable, Auntie backed out of the driveway.

Rock Junior High was quite literally a stone's throw away, situated on the next block between Ohio and Summit Avenue. Auntie drove around the one-way blocks and parked along Tenth Street in front of the upper school building.

"Don't get in there and show your behind with these teachers," she said. "This ain't none of St. Ann."

"Yes, ma'am."

There were three buildings. The one that housed the seventh graders was a century old, with peeling lead-based paint and exposed uninsulated pipes resembling an open-bay prison block. A newly erected gymnasium, fashioned out of prefabricated metal, sat between that and the thirties-era redbrick upper school.

We walked up a flight of stairs to the principal's office. The hallways were oddly silent, but the thing I remember most was the pervasive odor of piss and mildew. The roof of the entry hall was leaking. A janitor was busy mopping up a puddle around a white paint bucket.

Inside the office, we were greeted by a woman wearing large hoop earrings and bright red lipstick. Auntie Gerald stepped to the counter and announced herself. She dutifully handed over my birth certificate and final report card from Hoech.

"She's a gifted child," she said as the school secretary inspected the report card. "Straight As, up and down the line."

"I see. And she's coming from Ritenour Schools in St. Louis County?"

Auntie nodded and smiled.

"Tell me, young lady, what was the last book you read."

"Homer."

"Homer who?"

"He doesn't have a last name. Homer is a Greek poet. The last book I finished was *The Odyssey*. I'm reading *The Iliad* now."

"And what is that about?"

"Soldiers and wars, mostly," I said.

"You have nice diction."

Auntie Gerald nodded, approvingly, and said, "She's been reading since she was three years old. She skipped kindergarten at Longfellow."

"I don't see her standardized test scores here. We will send for the transcripts. In the meantime, she'll be assigned to Peggy LeCompte's homeroom. It's just downstairs, right below us. The class is going to Algebra I now with Mr. Forehand. I see here that you've already taken algebra, young lady."

"Yes, ma'am, and some geometry."

"I don't see that on your report card."

"I've been teaching myself out my sister's math book."

She nodded and said, "Mrs. Ross, I assume you have proof of residency?"

Auntie Gerald handed over the papers to her house.

"We own our home," she continued.

I suppose she wanted the secretary to know that we were good people, people who went to work every day and owned rather than rented. She did not mention, of course, that I had no mattress and that I slept head-to-foot with my cousins on the living room floor. There was no mention of the rationed food, the not so infrequent floggings, or that my mother was living with a man in a comfortable townhouse up the highway.

She never asked where my mother was and there was no mention of guardianship papers. A burly lump of a man came in and leaned sideways against the counter. He scanned through some documents, eyed me with a mix of curiosity and suspicion, said nothing and left.

The school secretary escorted me up a flight of stairs to Mr. Forehand's math class. He was standing at the chalkboard, fiddling over a multivariate polynomial equation, when I entered. Forehand was looking for a taker and finding none.

"Come on, someone tell me what's y."

I looked around the room and said, "It's seven."

"Very good. Now, come here and show me why. What's your name?"

"Goldie."

"Is that a nickname?"

"No, it's the one my mother gave me."

That got a laugh from Johnny, a brutish eighth grader.

"She's my cousin," Claire interjected, before anybody else could pile on.

We weren't actually related, but we'd known one another since we were toddlers. And, I suppose, Claire was issuing a bit of a warning. She was, after all, bigger than most of the boys and she had a pair of six-foot-tall sisters at home.

There were more familiar faces, children I'd known from around our block. Still, even with older cousins attending both Lincoln and East Side and a younger one in the seventh-grade building, I was largely alone. I wasn't used to the turmoil between bells in the hallways or the chaos that erupted once the dismissal bell sounded. A fight between two boys broke out in the hallway. We were only in eighth grade, but it was the most vicious and violent thing I had ever witnessed. Blood spilled on the floor.

The other girls in school wore their hair in pretty, hot-combed hairstyles or expensive Jheri curls. They had name-brand tennis shoes and one even had a gold tooth. A boy in my last class leaned over and said I had pretty eyes. I smiled and said thank you.

"Too bad your face don't go with them," he said, laughing.

A small crowd joined in, giggling and pointing at everything they thought was wrong with me and my clothes.

"Leave me alone."

"Shut up, you nappy-headed bitch."

I felt my face redden, but I refused to cry.

By the time we cycled back into homeroom, I was distraught. I was stunned by the generalized coarseness. When the dismissal bell rang, I ran straight home and locked myself in Grandma Alice's room.

"What's wrong, Golleh?"

"I'm ugly," I said. "My hair, my clothes and everything."

"Hush y'self," Grandma Alice said, taking a seat beside

me. "You looked nice when you left outta here this morning. Maybe Geraldine can take you over to see Miss Shirley."

Shirley Starr was the family hairdresser. She had a salon in her basement, around the corner from Auntie Killer's house. It was decked out with standing hair drying and pressing combs. A hand-printed, misspelled sign on the wall listed the services and prices. Grandma Alice said she'd pay for me to go every other Saturday with Auntie Gerald.

"Go on now," she said, giving me a deep, long hug. "See after your chores and your homework. You don't need no more trouble. I'll talk to Geraldine."

Mrs. LeCompte arrived late the next morning. It was after nine thirty and the teacher from the classroom next door, Mrs. Reece, had been sent to attend to us. Tamiko, a bowl-headed girl with a broad smile, was holding court in a bank of desks behind me, furtively prattling on until the room suddenly fell silent. Her attention snapped toward the door.

"I beg your pardon, Miss Youngblood," Mrs. LeCompte said with a scoff.

Tamiko grew wide-eyed. She sat down quietly, ashamed to be caught unawares.

I watched the short round woman march to her desk, slip off her high heels and put on her satin house shoes. Without so much as a good morning, she went to the chalkboard and wrote out a lengthy, compound-complex sentence in perfect cursive.

"Take out a piece of paper and diagram this sentence," she said evenly.

There was a collective grumble. The string of dependent and independent clauses, replete with compound adjectives and adverbs and objects of prepositions, linked together by conjunctions, was mind-numbing. Mrs. LeCompte folded her arms, paced the room, and waited.

I struggled through the sections at first, scribbling and erasing until I landed on a reasonable construct. When I finished, I laid down my pencil and let my thoughts roam about the room. It was a large space, decorated in bright colors, its walls lined with laminated pictures of famous Black people and motivational platitudes on oversize placards.

"Are you finished?"

"Yes."

She waved me to the front of the room and handed me the chalk. I was having second thoughts about my graph. I hesitated.

"Well, let's see it."

I started drawing, using my paper as a guide. I quickly ran out of space.

"Erase it and start again. Start with a plan."

I carefully mapped out the sentence and neatly labeled each of the sectors.

"Very good, Miss Taylor. Take your seat."

It went on like that for several weeks, with Mrs. LeCompte challenging the class with tough questions and me calling out answers from the back of the room, until I walked into homeroom one morning and found that she'd rearranged the desks in a square so there was no back row. She placed me in the one closest to her desk, a favored spot customarily reserved for whoever was in the most trouble that day.

"Did I do something wrong?" I asked. "Why do I have to sit here?"

"Because this is my classroom and I make the rules."

I suspect she knew I was helping two boys sitting on either side of me with their work. As long as I did that, they kept the bullies at bay.

Mrs. LeCompte rewarded my studious nature by picking me to lead class projects and gave me side work when she realized I had finished the day's assignments.

Socially awkward and all but fully enculturated by life in a white, working-class suburb, I rushed through the day's assignments and didn't speak unless called on. Soon, though, I came to understand that I was never going to be teased for being smart. There were no wayward cousins around to berate and pester, and nobody made fun of my appetite for English poets or the way I overenunciated my words. When the bell rang that morning, Mrs. LeCompte pulled me aside and handed me a copy of "Invictus" by William Ernest Henley.

"I want you to memorize this," she said, "and be ready to recite it Friday."

I had no idea why I had been given the task, but I was enamored by the poem. It felt powerful and I was enlivened by the language.

> *Out of the night that covers me,*
> *Black as the pit from pole to pole,*
> *I thank whatever gods may be*
> *For my unconquerable soul.*

I'd never encountered anything quite like it before. At home, I paced the floor, mumbling the lines to myself, until I had them down pat. By the third day, I was adding emphasis to some of the words and changing the cadence in my voice.

> *It matters not how strait the gate,*
> *How charged with punishments the scroll,*
> *I am the master of my fate,*
> *I am the captain of my soul.*

I repeated the last line twice, as if Henley had somehow made a mistake. I felt triumphant holding court in front of the bathroom mirror, like I had the full of the world in my hands.

"Save some of that for church," Auntie Gerald called out from her bedroom. "You sound good."

That Friday morning, I walked to the front of the class. The room seemed to disappear as I stepped up to the center of the room in front of the chalkboard. Mrs. LeCompte raised her hands. The room came to a hush.

"You may begin," she said, nodding.

I launched in immediately. At times booming, there was an urgency in my voice. When it was over, the class applauded. Mrs. LeCompte was pleased. She handed copies to everyone, with the same assignment.

"You have one week," she said.

Walking the short distance from Auntie Gerald's house to school was like stepping into the aftermath of a war zone every morning. The grounds were surrounded by dilapidated buildings and the feeder streets were fraught with hazards. Broken glass and empty-eyed addicts dotted the crumbling roadways. Sewage sometimes backed up into the street, and the city's garbage workers seemed to go on strike and never come back. Every other afternoon, fights erupted just outside the schoolyard.

If things got bad, as they sometimes did, invariably somebody would pick up a brick or a piece of broken cinder block. With kids hurling chunks of concrete, wood planks, and metal poles wedged from abandoned buildings, it wasn't unusual for somebody's mama to jump in it, especially if that somebody's mama was just on the other side of high school age herself. In fact, most of the kids I went to school with had at least one parent who was under thirty years old, and it wouldn't be long before they would be grandparents themselves.

The police never showed up. That was mostly because there weren't enough working squad cars and radios to police the streets. Brawls kept going until somebody ran off bleeding or got tired of swinging.

Auntie Gerald was not oblivious to the risks. I had to be home by three thirty-five, or exactly five minutes after the final bell rang. I was warned, more than once, not to fool around with kids who didn't live on our block and to stay out of the Gompers. A girl we knew had been dragged into an abandoned apartment, sexually assaulted, and left for dead.

The framed houses and well-appointed bungalows that once lined the avenues were gone now, gutted by fire or neglect, and reduced to bricks. What was a prosperous, blue-collar town booming with industry from its stockyards, meat processing plants, restaurants, banks, and shopping district was now dissolving into financial chaos. The Sears department store that used to anchor the corner of State Street and Tenth had been gutted and reconstructed to house the school district offices.

The area in and around East St. Louis, I came to learn, was referred to by geographers as "the American Bottom." The problems ran deeper than vacant houses, shuttered factories, and de-annexation. The entire city sat on a flood plain, which, even with the levees, made redevelopment all but unfeasible. But for that, Auntie Gerald said, they might've bulldozed East St. Louis a long time ago.

"Only people that stay here are people who ain't got no way to leave."

Despite its lack of resources, tumbledown buildings and the hurdles children faced at home and on the street, Rock and the other four lower secondary schools were an athletic proving ground. Families transferred into District 189 so their children could train in track, cross-country, basketball, volleyball, and football. If you played one varsity sport, you were expected to play three.

Across the district, basketball teams, both girls and boys, practiced on Sundays. Only players whose parents verified they were in church got a pass. My cousin Bernadette regularly called the head basketball coach at Lincoln Senior High because her son was singing baritone in the choir at Mt. Perion every first and fourth Sunday. If Jesus was our family's first religion, then sports were a close second. We prayed over pole vaults and slam dunks like plates of collards and black-eyed peas. For Bernadette's boy and so many others, the only ticket out was a college athletic scholarship, the back of a squad car or the morgue.

The East Side Flyers, a high school football dynasty led by Coach Bob Shannon, won multiple state championships on nothing but discipline and grit. In one five-year span, they never lost a single game. Running out a ninety-yard touch-down run was routine. Once profiled in a segment on CBS *60 Minutes*, there were years when District 189 didn't have enough money to wash the team's uniforms and the squad showed up for championship games with holes in the seats of their pants. They won anyway. The Flyers were considered so formidable that opponents sometimes chose to forfeit rather than show up to play. If an opposing squad did manage to beat a team from East St. Louis, they had to be escorted back to their buses.

Even as the township itself deteriorated down to hollowed-out husks, there were so many sports stars coming out of those schools and so many state titles that city leaders adopted the moniker "City of Champions." It was printed in large red letters on a gigantic billboard erected in an open field down the street from Auntie Gerald's house, so the cars traveling the interstate highway could see it. If there is one thing to be said about that sign, it is this: what the city lacked in money and means, it more than made up for with its willingness to fight. Most often, it was a point of respect. Sports was its own religion in East St. Louis, but everybody we knew had a "church home."

★ ★ ★

Houses of worship, from towering cathedrals to storefront congregations, churches outnumbered the liquor stores and Chinese rice houses. Our family belonged to Mt. Perion, a church so backward that they even gave it the wrong name. When the church anniversary came around every year, invariably somebody would point out that nobody could find a Mt. Perion in the Bible. I found the real name, Mt. Paran, and pointed it out to Auntie Gerald. When she told Reverend Hubbard about it, he refused to change it. So, my aunt, who was the Sunday school superintendent, put me in charge of the children's class.

Every first and fourth Sunday, the rest of my cousins and me dressed up in black skirts and slacks and pressed white shirts to belt out various hymns. I was placed on the far end of the front row of the choir stand. To the delight of the Mother's Board, a group of women elders, I was given a solo in the song "Because He Lived." I sounded like a winding crankshaft when a car starter won't catch.

Church had always been a major aspect of our lives. Auntie Gerald believed in "training children up" and I was no exception. I leaned hard on that faith now. Outside of school, this was the one place where I was celebrated. Old women from the Mother's Board pressed folded dollar bills into my hands and often told me how special I was. Brother John Griggs, the head deacon, and his wife, Sister Anna, doted on me like I was one of their own. They wanted to know about my grades and what I was learning in school. It was not uncommon for Sister Griggs to stop and straighten my skirt or slide me an extra slice of cake at the church banquet. I had been baptized by Reverend Jonah Hubbard in '74, a few months after my father was murdered, only because the pastor kept making it sound like we all needed to hurry up and get right before Jesus came back.

"We know not the day, nor the hour!"

So, on the fourth Sunday of March, after the benediction had been recited and service was letting out, I wiggled through a bevy of sweet-smelling women and walked up to Pastor Hubbard. I tugged on his black cassock and told him I wanted to get baptized.

I suppose the mere sight of a five-and-a-half-year-old professing a lifelong faith in Christ was too much for Sister Griggs, who sold Beeline clothes out of catalogs and had her own line of hats. What I remember most about Sister Griggs, though, was her always perfect pressed and curled hair and the way her pearly white dentures contrasted with her deep cocoa complexion. She hauled around a pocketbook that seemed to carry an endless supply of butterscotch candies, another reason I adored her. That morning, Sister Griggs wept and shouted hallelujah, over and over, until folks started passing out in the pews.

I was baptized the next week following the Lord's Supper, a communion of unsalted crackers and Welch's grape juice we observed every fifth Sunday. My mother put me in a plastic swimming cap and the machine-stitched white frock she spent all week making from a cut-up bedsheet.

One Sunday morning between services, I was sitting on the living room floor with a novel when Auntie Gerald walked in and kicked off her church shoes.

"What're you reading?"

"A book."

"I know it's a dern book. What's it about?"

"A plane crashed and some boys got stuck on an island. Now, they're trying to hunt for food."

"Hand it here."

Auntie Gerald slipped the paperback from my hands and plopped down on a tufted Queen Anne chair. She pushed her eyeglasses up the bridge of her nose and studied the cover.

"*Lord of the Flies*, huh?"

"Yes, ma'am. There's a boy named Piggy in the book, just like Lori."

"LeCompte give you this?"

"No, ma'am. It's Pig's," I said, calling Lori Ann by the nickname she hated. "She left it at our house in St. Ann."

I had a good many of my sister's old schoolbooks. After Lori Ann left for college and got married, I found them tucked into the bottom of our closet. I'd already read her American and world history books and done the quizzes after the chapters. By then, I was working my way through her algebra and geometry books.

"How many more of these you got?"

"Five or six."

"And how long do it take you to read the whole thing?"

"I don't know. I guess a week."

"I'll tell you what," she said. "Every time you read one of these, you write me a book report and you don't have to wash dishes every Sunday."

I smiled.

"I can do that."

I quickly figured out that, if I kept my nose buried in a book of some sort, Auntie Gerald would let up on me. I still couldn't leave our block and, on the weekends, I had to be in the house before the streetlights came on. When she wasn't home, either off shopping up the highway or at her bridge club meetings, we had to stay inside until she got back.

"Too much going on out here in these streets," she said.

14

I wasn't the first or the last Robinson child to go to Rock. Though mostly of the school-skipping, pot-smoking variety, there had been cousins, distant and claimed, and my own siblings. Some graduated, while others took another road in life. Such was the case with Bug, who got pregnant, dropped out and later earned a GED.

Between the asbestos insulation, lead-based paint, turn-of-the-century plumbing and unstable foundation, Rock was a standing public health threat. But the city couldn't afford to replace it or any of the others.

When I got there, Mrs. LeCompte was still running the gifted program, as she had been when my sister, Lori Ann, was in her class. She taught advanced English from the same textbook I'd used the previous year in St. Ann. The school had no gateway testing to discern whether a student met basic criteria for the accelerated track. I quickly came to understand that getting in meant next to nothing in a school system that performed far below state and national standards. Reading on or near grade level seemed to be enough.

If I thought the classwork in a school that didn't have enough textbooks to go around would be easy, I was wrong. Mrs. LeCompte pushed to me to my academic limits. John Forehand, a wiry white man with oil-slicked dark hair, turned out to be one of the most brilliant math teachers I ever encountered. Rock didn't offer Algebra II, so Mr. Forehand started giving me extra assignments. I stayed after school two or three times a week to work on problems with him.

Although another teacher, Gerold Nave, chided me for not working hard enough.

"You don't even take your history book home," he said, pointing at me one afternoon.

I looked up from a book. He raised his brow as if to say, *Yes, I am talking to you.*

While he was in the middle of one his classroom sermons about the virtues of hard work and convenient trouble, figuring it didn't have anything to do with me, I skimmed a Baldwin novel, hoping it would pass. Somehow, though, even with a renowned miscreant sitting behind me at the time, I had become Nave's target. It was the second-to-last period of the day and Nave, who doubled as the girls' track coach, wasn't happy to find me reading a novel as he taught class.

Nave would not be ignored. When he wasn't decked out in purple-and-white sweats, he wore three-piece suits with a chained gold watch in the waist pocket and walked around with an unlit walnut pipe in his mouth. Nave was a former high school football standout at East St. Louis Senior High and graduated in '64 before going on to Southern Illinois University at Edwardsville. He earned a Masters in Social Studies from Webster University and a second in Education Administration from SIU. Others went to Fisk, Lincoln University of Missouri, Tennessee State, and Harris-Stowe. He taught US history and, unlike the other classes, this one mostly entailed completing some fill-in-the-blank worksheets and the occasional film strip.

"What do you have to say for yourself?"

"About what?"

"When're you going to start putting in some effort?"

"I finish my work before we get out."

"Then do the next assignment and the next one after that."

"Why would I wanna do that?"

"Don't get mad, get better. Prove me wrong, young lady."

"Give me something to work on and I'll do it."

When he turned back to the chalkboard, presumably to write down a new assignment, I reopened the book and continued reading. Nave spun around on his heels.

"Give it to me and go to the office."

"What for?"

"Insubordination," he said. "You know what that means?"

"What rule did I break? You didn't give me any directions to be insubordinate about."

"I'm not going to argue with you. Get out."

I gathered my satchel, found my way downstairs to the office, and told the secretary why I was there. She frowned.

"You know better," she sighed. "What book was it?"

"*Go Tell It on the Mountain.*"

"James Baldwin?"

"Yes, ma'am."

"Have a seat."

She got on the P.A. system and called down to my home-room. The secretary, Mrs. LeCompte and Principal Howell huddled in his office, then waved me inside. Mr. Howell started in.

"What seems to be the problem, young lady?"

"I finished my work and Mr. Nave wasn't teaching anything. Anyway, I did all this last year. I don't see why I have to do it again."

"That may well be, but let me be clear, Miss Taylor," Mrs. LeCompte said. "We have rules here and you will be expected to follow them. Did you get the book from the library?"

"No, ma'am," I said. "It's my sister's."

"You will apologize to Mr. Nave."

"Yes, ma'am."

"And I expect to see a book report. Five hundred words. Tomorrow," Mrs. LeCompte said. "I do not have to tell you that it should be perfect. I want to see some sweat on the page."

"Well, then it would be wet."

"Do not get smart with me. I am not Mr. Nave."

Before I could catch myself, I said, "Well, he *is* bald."

Her eyes snapped like a pair of firecrackers. Mrs. LeCompte was a woman of severe discipline. She appeared each day, immaculately dressed and ready for war. Her classroom was her personal battlefield, and she was the general. She drove a beautiful cream-white car with vanity plates that said AKA 14, a reference to the Alpha Kappa Alpha sorority. She was the chapter president, among other lofty positions she held in the community, and penned a weekly society column in the *East St. Louis Monitor* newspaper. Exquisitely and proudly Black, LeCompte was revered by her colleagues and feared by every student in her orbit.

"One more time," the principal interjected, "and I will let Mr. McKnuckles deal with you and call Mrs. Ross up here."

It was a threat I didn't take lightly. I was terrified that Auntie Gerald might have to come up to the school. Mc-Knuckles hadn't had a turn with me yet, but I'd seen what he did to other children. If things got out of hand, as they so often did, Assistant Principal McKnuckles was always at the ready. He patrolled the halls with a wooden paddle and frequently whacked children for even the most minor infractions. He was a burly man with hard features and skin as black as motor oil, who seemed to take pleasure in meting out swats. His name remains one of life's great ironies. Teachers called for him like ordering takeout. It wasn't unusual to see kids lined up in the hall, waiting their turn for a paddling.

I finally did something to draw his ire. I took a thrashing from McKnuckles when I didn't produce my hall pass quickly enough. I started crying, and he walked away laughing. I went right home and told Uncle Ross, who, unbeknownst to Auntie Gerald, threatened to knock him on his ass if he ever touched me again.

In Mrs. LeCompte's homeroom, we were sequestered and worked out like prizefighters. The differing standards for the gifted track, or the Talented Tenth, as they called us, and the rest of the student body were stark. While we were given rigorous lessons and pushed toward extracurricular activities that would prepare us for Advanced Placement courses in high school, those deemed unreachable were fed with film strips and what amounted to coloring sheets to pass the time.

After my turn with "Invictus," she handed me Margaret Walker's "For My People." Again, I was enamored. She wasn't British like Henley, but Black like me. Again, I did not question the assignment. I simply went to work. It took me a bit longer to memorize the stanzas but, again, the words spoke to me in a way that nothing else had.

There were no natural breaks, no place to take a breath unless I made one, and it was decidedly baked in an anguish that I could relate to.

In memory of the bitter hours when we discovered we
were black and poor and small and different and nobody
cared and nobody wondered and nobody understood.

Walker was all at once sad and furious. But there was hope in the lines, hope I could not bring myself to embrace.

Let a new earth rise. Let another world be born. Let a
bloody peace be written in the sky.

I understood, then, that I was getting an education that none of the others was being afforded, something above and beyond what even my classmates received. I felt both special and alone. Nave kept poking at me, pressing me to do even more.

"The only limit you have is the one in your head," he said, tapping me on the temple.

Back in our old town, a single-parent-led household like ours had been an anomaly. I didn't know of any foster children back at Buder or Hoech, although I am sure there were some, and only a smattering of children got free or reduced lunch. By comparison, nearly early every student at Rock reported some level of welfare dependency and, thus, qualified for the federally subsidized free-lunch program. For some of the children, the only full meal they had was a school lunch and sometimes it came premade in plastic wrappers. Sometimes the shipments never made it there. Trucks carrying cafeteria supplies and stocks of food were routinely robbed. There was the added complexity of growing up in a city where the homicide rate once topped nineteen times the national average.

Gunfire was a nightly occurrence in the projects and often spilled into the surrounding neighborhoods. Over in the Gompers, the kids knew to take cover in the bathtub if gunfire sounded close. We didn't answer knocks at the door, especially at night, if we weren't expecting company.

The worse things got, the more people who were hauled off to jail or to the morgue, the more restrictions Auntie Gerald laid on the children who crossed her threshold. In so many ways, she was building a world within a world, one separate and apart from the chaos that reigned outside. But the house that was supposed to be a shelter had its own dangers. For all of the physical precautions she took to keep me safe, little or no attention was paid to the war going on inside me. I was a walking wreckage. Angry most of the time, I resented everything that breathed. Other than church, I generally kept to myself. I had few friends, like Deborah, and that was fine by me.

What I understand most about the teaching team now is that they attempted to meet students where they were and, in their minds, that meant a bifurcated education. It was the "soft bigotry of low expectations," as former President George W. Bush put it. But for the fundamental unfairness of tracking, some children who might have otherwise thrived never saw their full potential in bloom.

That type of education takes resources, girded by a strong tax base, to recruit and fully equip a faculty more vigorously prepared to support students who underperform or present with challenges driven by outside environments. However, it should be said now that Bush-era policy ideas such as No Child Left Behind and "school choice" were unfunded platitudes that deepen divides rather than cure them.

Whatever their methods, training or rationale, the teachers at Rock were interested in one thing: giving Black children a fighting chance. For some students, that meant getting a basketball scholarship to a state university or entry into the dual enrollment program at the local community college. For others, that merely meant a marginally safe place to be every day and something halfway decent to eat.

District budgets didn't allow for in-school counselors, and a box of Band-Aids was the only nurse on duty. There were children in severe need of wraparound social services, kids like Boss Man, whose parents wouldn't or couldn't show up for teacher conferences. The only therapy available was Mr. McKnuckles's well-worn paddle.

The children in my classes came from a variety of circumstances, and most of them weren't good. There were at least six foster care children in my eighth-grade homeroom alone, maybe more, something I had never heard of before. There were those who lived with both parents, but several were under the care of a grandparent, and four that I knew of had at least one incarcerated parent or older sibling.

My friend Deborah, who I came to love like a sister and who had a singing voice the angels would envy, was a foster child and lived across the alley with the candy lady, Mrs. Ferguson. Generally soft-spoken until she opened her mouth to sing, Deborah was a popular girl with a soft heart who got along with everybody. One day in the choir room, as we rearranged the chairs and tidied up, our small talk turned serious.

"Do you ever wanna go back?" Deborah asked me once, referring to St. Ann.

"Sometimes I do, sometimes I don't."

"What's it like living around all those white people?"

"Different."

Talking about St. Ann and the life I'd left behind made me uneasy. I didn't ask about her mother, and she didn't ask about mine.

"They say you got raped."

I expected to feel something. I didn't. I had not spoken a word to anybody about that night. By then, though, I'd as-

sumed just that everybody knew. But hearing it come out of
Deborah's mouth still hit differently.

"Who is *they*?"

"You know how people talk. You alright?"

I shrugged.

"Ain't nothing that ain't never happened to nobody else,"
I said.

Deborah was confused. Not by what I said, but how I
said it.

I rarely used slang. Before I moved in with Auntie Gerald, I
really didn't know how. My cousin Bug said the problem was
I thought I was better than everybody else. But these days, I
was starting to sound a lot like her. Emotionally, I was hard-
ening. And, just like Bug, it got so that I'd swing on somebody before I'd drop a tear.

"Did he go to jail?"

"No."

"We can't change what happened to us," she said.

I knew then that she had been assaulted, too, though she
never said specifically. She never talked about where she came
from, but Deborah and I had a lot in common. That included
Darnell, who was her foster cousin.

"Do you mind if I pray?"

"For what?"

"For us."

I nodded. Deborah took my hands and started praying. It
was a beautiful thing, I thought at the time. I was impressed
that somebody her age could pray like a grown woman.

When she was finished, I raised my head and said, "I guess I needed somebody to tell me it's going to be alright."

"Trouble don't last always."

"I wish I could sing like you."

"I can't fix that, but I can teach you how to pray."

HOW HIGH THE MOON

15

I wanted more time with Baldwin.

Not the man with the pretty words printed in books, but the one who showed me a deeper reflection of the world than I had ever known. I wanted to meet him in person, to know him, to talk to him. I wanted to sit in his apartment on Seventy-First Street in New York and drink wine and carry on like old friends. I wanted to tell him about myself and listen as his smoke-cracked voice walked me through all of my tomorrows.

When I decided to write a second Baldwin essay, this one about the author rather than one of his books, Mrs. LeCompte agreed to give me extra credit, provided the work was "flawless." Penning a biographical piece would prove more difficult. Source material was scant. There were no texts about him in what passed for a school library. I had Auntie's set of encyclopedias, and though there were a few relevant paragraphs about other Black writers, scientists, and abolitionists, I found nary a trace of Baldwin. Instead, I found plenty about Charles Drew and Harriet Tubman and the "right kind of Negroes" as Uncle Ross put it.

The only public library in town was three blocks up on the corner of Ninth and State Street. Mrs. LeCompte said there was a decent newspaper archive, but I needed permission from the head librarian to see it. Like everything else, though, except the liquor stores, Chinese rice houses, and nightclubs, it closed early and there wasn't a single bookstore in the city. Since my daily curfew was three thirty-five every afternoon, I had to ask Uncle Ross to take me. He hunted around for his keys, slipped on a button-down shirt, and said, "Let's go."

"Right now?"

"You wanna go, don't you? Hurry on and get your shoes."

I'd seen Baldwin on television once. It was some late-night talk show, I think. He and Uncle Ross looked oddly alike, only Baldwin was a slight man. Not so similar as to pass for brothers, but close enough to be cousins. Unlike my uncle, Baldwin seemed angry, but in a devil-may-care sort of way and concerned himself with the problems of the Negro. I was angry, too, though of the boiling variety, I suppose. Uncle Ross was a more genteel spirit, whose chief concerns were keeping me in line, the house in good order, and making sure his dogs ate that day.

My uncle sat outside in the Buick while I scoured the aisles for anything about Baldwin. The microfiche archive was a marvelous thing, just as Mrs. LeCompte promised. I kept going outside to make sure I still had time, until Uncle finally gave in and said he'd come back at closing time. He made me promise not to leave the building.

When I finally set about writing one night, I had little to go on outside of a few stories about Baldwin I'd found on microfiche films.

"People cry easier than they can change," he'd told a *New York Times* reporter in 1977.

I'd dropped and seen enough tears to know that was true. It was easier, I knew, to shoot myself in the head than fight off the madness still bubbling inside.

"James Baldwin is missing," the opening line said.

The essay went on for more than a thousand words, written in cursive in a spiral-bound notebook in the dim of the kitchen. The keys on Auntie's old manual typewriter stuck and the black-and-red ribbon was dried out, but Mrs. LeCompte never liked excuses or the people who made them. So I wrote the essay by hand. She encouraged the use of a thesaurus, and demanded that each handwritten page be legible and error free.

At times surly and dismissive, I was always in trouble of some sort, and my punishment was invariably more writing. As the exercises kept coming, the nights grew longer. This time, though, the assignment was one of my own making. LeCompte, I'm sure, had to know how much I enjoyed it.

I hovered over a *World Book*, straining to read the passages under a grayish glow from the fluorescent light over the sink. I scribbled notes about the white writers I found and Black writers I had not. I decided to title it "In Search of Baldwin." It was well past midnight when Bernadette's man-child found me there.

"You better do them dishes before Grandma Gerald finds out."

"I stay in trouble."

"What for?"

"Reading all the time. Mostly in Mr. Nave's class."

"That's stupid."

"Reading in class or getting into trouble for it?"

"Both. That's dumb."

"So are you."

"I'm smarter than you."

"You should wish. You lucky Nave don't make you run black lines in the gym like he do us."

"I guess that makes me smarter and luckier than you."

"Grandmamma know?"

"No, and if you tell her I'm going to tell her about that girl. Anyway, this isn't punishment. I wanted to do it."

"Who would want to do that?"

"Somebody smarter than you."

"Keep thinking that. What girl is you talking about anyway?"

"You know what girl I'm talking about."

"Let me see that," he said, pulling my notebook away.

"Give it back."

"You gone tell?"

"I don't care about you, and I sho'nug don't care about that girl."

"You talk too damn much. I got something that'll keep your mouth shut."

He tossed the book on the table and disappeared.

"Mangy, cock-eyed bastard," I said to myself.

I reopened my notebook and copied a passage from Baldwin's novel *Go Tell It on the Mountain.*

"Looking at his face, it sometimes came to her that all women had been cursed from the cradle," it said, "all, in one fashion or another, being given the same cruel destiny, born to suffer the weight of men."

Baldwin made things make sense. He was a ready salve, meeting me at my point of need.

"Crime became real, for example—for the first time—not as *a* possibility but as *the* possibility. One would never defeat one's circumstances by working and saving one's pennies; one would never, by working, acquire that many pennies, and, besides, the social treatment accorded even the most successful Negroes proved that one needed, in order to be free, something more than a bank account."

The profundity of it all, of Baldwin's writings and, then later, of Dr. King's, was at once searing, jarring, and comforting. I had read Jane Austen for the thrill of it, for the excitement of traveling to some faraway land where I could escape my circumstances. To the contrary, in his "Letter From a Religion in My Mind," published by the *New Yorker* in 1962, Baldwin spoke to the horrors that I had witnessed and known for myself. Violence, as Baldwin described, was no esoteric notion. It was the daily reality of our lives.

One night, a half-naked man had come through Auntie's second back door off the dining room, which we were used to leaving unlocked. We were watching television in the dark when he stumbled in with his ding-a-ling swinging. Small and as black as a coal briquette, he seemed to be confused about where he was. My uncle didn't waste time asking what he wanted.

He dipped into the kitchen, emerged with a butcher knife, and waved it over his head.

"Get on outta here, you hear!"

As the man backed out slowly with his palms in the air, Uncle Ross slammed the door shut. He then went around, room to room, checking all the windows and doors. The next day, he got out his tools and installed metal brackets and a wood crossbar over that door and the one leading into the basement from outside. Soon, iron burglar bars were purchased for all of the lower windows, and locking metal screen doors were hung at the front and back entrances.

Uncle Ross never owned a gun that I knew of, but the house felt like a fortress. Between Auntie Gerald's tirades about whatever was out in the street and Uncle Ross's grandson lurking around the house at night, it was safer in school than out.

I did not see us as entirely separate and apart, as my aunt and uncle almost certainly did. While I still harbored a deep and abiding antipathy for Ronnie Lee and Bug then, I began to consider us and even the man who broke into Auntie's house, as Baldwin did, all paddling the same boat.

"Perhaps we were, all of us—pimps, whores, racketeers, church members, and children—bound together by the nature of our oppression, the specific and peculiar complex of risks we had to run," Baldwin wrote.

While Auntie Gerald said we should pray over all God's children, Uncle Ross was ready to take an eye for an eye. If that man had made a single threatening move, I have no doubt Uncle Ross would've split him open on the spot.

On what was supposed to be a quiet Sunday evening, in late March of that year, I sat on the stairs busying myself with a magazine. The television blared in the background.

"Gerald! Gerald! Come look at this!" Grandma Alice called out.

The evening news was on. The owner of Slay's Restaurant had been murdered. Two busboys, both twenty years old, were being charged with killing Tony Slay. They'd stolen the dead man's car and meat from the freezer, but missed $1,700 in cash, tucked inside his coat pocket when they bludgeoned him to death with a billy club. The murder weapon, found days later, had belonged to Slay's son, a former St. Louis police officer.

The news was riddled with such stories, but this one rocked our house. I watched as my uncle and aunt gathered around the television set, fixated and wistful at the images of the body being loaded into a coroner's wagon.

The Slays, a prominent family of Lebanese immigrants, were some of the first restaurant owners to serve Black people, Uncle Ross explained. Tony Slay's brother, Francis, was a political power broker. Serving two terms as the city's recorder of deeds, multiple terms in the Missouri House, and as the Democratic committeeman for the Twenty-Third Ward, he was the putative dean of St. Louis Democrats.

"Lord, have mercy, Jesus," Grandma Alice said.

Uncle Ross sighed and said, "What we doing to ourselves?"

It was assumed, although I never knew for certain, that the assailants were Black. Auntie Gerald blamed it on drugs. Jodie Peoples, the shirtless gangbanger who lived behind us, was dealing off his daddy's front porch.

Life in East St. Louis was changing quickly then. The threads holding the town together seemed to snap. There were more home invasions and armed robberies, driven by desperate addicts and a teetering economy. Amid mounting inflation and a national recession, the worst economic downturn since the Great Depression, people were losing jobs and food banks were overwhelmed. As drugs poured into the streets, criminal court dockets swelled.

Grandma Alice said it was Ronald Reagan's fault and Auntie Gerald talked about "trickle-down economics" like it was a bucket of hot piss. At church, Reverend Hubbard never preached about anything going on in Washington or down at City Hall. Black people, he said, were responsible for their own uplift and said God was our only answer.

"He's a doctor in the sick room and a lawyer in the courtroom!" he shouted from the pulpit.

I overheard one of the deacons say the CIA was dumping crack on the streets.

"They trying to kill us," Brother Griggs said. "Don't no colored man own no boats and airplanes. We ain't bringing none of that stuff in here."

Churches were not immune. Somebody broke into Mt. Perion. A thief got into the pastor's office up in the balcony and made off with the cash box. Somehow, the burglar was able to wedge the air conditioner out of the upper window. The portable units were often a target because they could be easily resold on the street.

With all the bars, new locks and metal screen doors, our house felt like a prison then. Nobody was allowed in or out unless Uncle Ross said so.

"I'm tired of being stuck in the house," I protested.

Auntie shrugged and said, "You ain't missing nothing out there."

16

Auntie Gerald usually did her grocery shopping on Saturday mornings. She almost never went to Nationals, a dim cavern of canned goods and fatty meats a few blocks away, preferring Schnuck's in Collinsville for lean meats and fresh vegetables. She sometimes stopped off at the Wonder Bread store, or a butcher shop up on State Street, where she waited her turn with her green stamps.

She collected S&H stamps from the cashier when she went to the market, based on the dollar amount of the purchase. The more you bought, the more you got. The perforated stickers had a gummy adhesive on the back so you could lick and affix them in rows on the pages of a small booklet. When Auntie had enough, she would trade them in for S&H catalog items. One year, she got a new set of pots and pans.

On a good week, she'd bring home a mess of big mouth buffalo belly, whole catfish, or crevalle jack for Uncle Ross to clean for Friday night supper. While I always thought eating fish on Friday had something to do with Jesus multiplying fish and loaves of bread, Auntie said we did it to honor the sacrifice of Christ.

"They hung him on that cross on a Friday," she said.

I still didn't know what that had to do with plates of jack spiked with hot sauce, but I gleefully dug in.

Dipped in a mixture of milk, eggs, and flour, she coated the fish in seasoned cornmeal, sometimes tail and all, before dropping the pieces into a sizzling pan of lard to go along with one-pot spaghetti and white bread. My uncle ate his on a sandwich with thick slices of pickle and onion, mustard, and hot sauce. He kept an aging, browning bottle of Tabasco in the pantry for such occasions.

Auntie Gerald had a lot of rules. Looking back now, I know she never ate with people she didn't like and didn't cook for nobody that she didn't love. Sundays meant stockpots of collard greens, sometimes fresh out of the field, stewed overnight with ham hocks with cuts of onion and Lawry's Seasoned Salt and a pan full of tucked, floured, and fried chicken wings. During the winter months, she brought home brown paper bags of peaches to slice into a pie and made deep-dish macaroni with hand-shaved cheddar cheese.

One Saturday, I waited for her to leave for the grocery store before I made my move. As the white Buick pulled out of the driveway, I dipped through the weeds and slipped across the back alley. On a previous gambit, I'd gotten a library card by forging Mama's signature. Booky once caught me coming back and gleefully blackmailed me into giving him the money I made from recycling aluminum cans so he could play pinball down at the corner store. In time, though, he started covering for me. Grandma Alice's closet was getting full now. Auntie Gerald adored the idea that I read a lot; she just didn't want her house cluttered with all the books. Everything had its place. Otherwise, it got tossed in the backyard firepit. That included library books I didn't have permission to go get in the first place.

The library on State Street, with its scant dusty shelves and rickety card catalog, wasn't anything near as nice or large as the one in St. Ann. It was, even if for a little while, a peaceful place to be. One Saturday morning, the clerk at the desk, a lady with sweet-smelling perfume and hot combed hair whose name I pray one day to remember, handed me a piece written by Frederick Douglass. It was a Xerox copy of the introduction he wrote for *The Reason Why the Colored American Is Not in the World's Columbian Exposition*, by Ida B. Wells.

"A ship rotting at anchor meets with no resistance," Frederick Douglass wrote, "but when she sets sail on the sea, she has to buffet opposing billows."

My questions were immediate and pressing. I rushed out of the house that Monday morning, dashing up the block and into school. Mrs. LeCompte wasn't there.

"Is she coming? Is she coming?"

"I'm afraid you're stuck with me today," said Miss Waters, the substitute.

"Can you help me with this?"

Miss Waters, who said she usually read three newspapers a day, had a rule: "Read it once for entertainment," she said, "and twice for understanding." She turned the question around and asked what I thought of it.

I shrugged.

Unfortunately, she looked a lot like her father, who taught a class of miscreants down the hall and regularly supervised in-school suspension. They had hard, broad features and wiry hair. Her typically dour expression softened with concern.

"'Conflict is better than stagnation,'" she said, quoting Douglass's final line.

"So, fight?"

"It takes courage to do the right thing. The fight is sometimes on the inside."

Back at home, Uncle Ross regularly skimmed the *St. Louis Post-Dispatch*. It was unusual to hear him talk about what was going on out in the world. With little in the way of a formal education, he tried to stand between us and the ugliness outside our front door. While Auntie checked up on my chores and made sure I kept myself clean, he urged me to fix my mind on my studies and to use my head before my fists. It should be said, though, that he taught me how to swing both.

He was never the kind to hand out gifts, so I was surprised when he got off the Edgemont bus on Summit Avenue one day with a copy of Alex Haley's *Autobiography of Malcolm X* under his arm.

"The man at the store didn't have anything by James Baldwin. I thought you'd like Brother Malcolm," he said, coming up the porch.

Black Liberation theology wasn't preached in our house. Malcolm X wasn't among the faces we celebrated during Black

History Month in school. I thanked Uncle Ross for the book, but it would be another year before I started reading it. His teachings were dangerous, I was told. Auntie Gerald couldn't abide by the notion that taking up arms would make things better for Black people.

"That mess ain't gone do nothing but get somebody killed," Auntie Gerald said. "That ain't God. Jesus don't need no gun to get his way."

My education to that point, both in St. Ann and at Rock, had been devoid of the inherent complexities of Civil Rights–era America, limited to King's nonviolent protests and Thurgood Marshall's work in the courtroom. It was around that time that I also discovered Dr. King's book *Where Do We Go from Here*.

"We have come a long way in our understanding of human motivation and of the blind operation of our economic system. Now we realize that dislocations in the market operation of our economy and the prevalence of discrimination thrust people into idleness and bind them in constant or frequent unemployment against their will," Dr. King wrote. "The poor are less often dismissed from our conscience today by being branded as inferior and incompetent. We also know that no matter how dynamically the economy develops and expands it does not eliminate all poverty."

There were things I didn't understand about King or, moreover, what was happening in the world around me. The distorted images I saw on the evening news and read about in Uncle Ross's newspapers made less sense when held under the light of Baldwin and King. The reality was, though, our lives were changing and almost none of it was good.

The raucous nighttime footraces up the avenue ended abruptly. The children around our block were now remanded to their homes at the first blink of the streetlights. An uneasy pall enveloped the streets in and around our Fifteenth and Exchange neighborhood when the sun went down. I remember, too, how the gunfire that often punctuated the silence changed. The once familiar ring of cheap pistols and booms from shotgun barrels was now replaced by the rapid pop of semiautomatics. The blasts sometimes erupted from moving cars, other times indiscriminately after high school basketball games.

Uncle Ross was quick to remind me that, if I worked hard and kept my nose clean, there was another life waiting for me. I didn't like being trapped inside. But I was old enough to know that wasn't always true, that a stray bullet after a school dance could change everything.

17

The first attack came in the basement on Thanksgiving night.

He shoved his fingers between my legs.

"You ain't on your period, is you?"

I shook my head no, squeezed my eyes shut and let the tears run down my face.

"Please don't."

"You know you like it. We ain't real cousins, anyway."

I screamed as he forced himself inside me. He grabbed me by the neck, gripping my jaw between his thumb and finger.

"Shut up," he said, pushing my legs over my shoulders.

I despised every single solitary thing about Uncle Ross's grandson, and, to this day, I have never hated anyone so deeply and so thoroughly. When he was done, he pulled up his gym shorts and left me in the basement. I lay there on the musty, mildewed bedspread and sobbed. I trembled. Waves of shame rushed over me.

I told no one. I couldn't bring myself to write about it in my journal. Putting words to that night would make them come alive again.

Even so, a few days later, I found charred pieces of my diary in the firepit out back. The remnants of the red plastic cover and its gold lock were among the ashes in the half-burned heap of garbage. I was immediately suspicious of Uncle Ross's grandson, who probably thought, like everything else in life, I'd written the whole thing down. Aunt Josie, after all, didn't run out the trash.

On the way to church that Sunday, Auntie Gerald hinted that she'd read the journal entries and set fire to the notebooks. Although I had not recounted what happened in the basement, there was page after page about Uncle Ross's grandson and every other terrible thing I encountered. For the most part, though, it read like a list of prayers. Deborah told me if I couldn't pray out loud, I should just tell God what I wanted. Books, new clothes and my own room were at the top.

"If you need to go to the library, Ross'll carry you up there, you hear?"

"Yes, ma'am."

Somebody had snitched on me for sneaking out on Saturday mornings. I looked at Booky. He shrugged his shoulders and threw a knowing glance at Uncle Ross's grandson.

Days later, I woke up with him on top of me one night. He put his hand over my mouth and shoved himself inside me. I bit his forearms, clamping down like a bear trap. I ran upstairs and dashed into Grandma Alice's room.

"Golley, you alright?"

"Yes, ma'am. Can I sleep with you?"

"As long as you go to the bathroom first."

I started making up reasons to stay after school and I hovered closer to Grandma Alice. I hung out in her room as she listened to the transistor radio or watched Max Robinson deliver the evening news on the downstairs television set. Sometimes, it meant feigning interest in opera house performances on PBS while she nodded on the sofa.

The attacks came closer and closer together. I felt like I was being hunted.

Around that time, Mr. McKnuckles stopped me in the hallway at school one day. I was walking back to the choir room after running an errand for our music teacher, Mrs. Bolden.

"Lemme see your hall pass."

I handed over the slip of paper with Mrs. Bolden's pretty cursive signature.

"Why do you walk around mad all the time, young lady?" he said, surveying the pass. His voice was deep and gruff, like he chewed on pebbles. "You look like a rattlesnake bit you in the face."

"Maybe one did," I snapped, before I could catch myself.

McKnuckles wasn't the kind to let such surliness slide, and I expected him to swat me on the backside.

"It can't be that bad," he said, with an unexpected drift of kindness.

I felt my face redden. Ashamed, I turned away toward the wall.

"Is it?"

"No, sir, it isn't."

"Look at me when I'm talking to you. Is it that bad?"

"No, sir, I'm okay."

"Go on back to class. Come and see me if somebody bothers with you."

"Yes, sir."

I turned to walk away.

"Say there, I heard you won that essay contest up in Belleville."

"Yes, sir, it was at the Optimist Club."

"Keep doing us proud, young lady."

I had performed "Please Hear What I'm Not Saying," a poem by Charles Finn. It was hard, at first, to grapple with the swell of emotion. It overtook me in waves and sometimes it was as if I was drowning in the words. For me, though, the recital was personal. It captured everything I had been through, saying everything I could not. I wanted to shout it from the rooftops.

…And so begins the parade of masks…
I tell you everything that's really nothing
And nothing of what's everything…

I wanted to tell somebody what my cousin was doing to me. Holding on to it felt like drinking poison. I was crouched in the corner of the quarter landing when I saw him coming up the stairs.

"Why you hiding?" he whispered.

"Fuck you," I sneered.

"Imma tell Grandma Gerald you up here cussing."

"Say something and I'm going to tell Uncle Ross what you did."

"No, you ain't. You like it and you know it."

"Keep fucking with me and watch."

"Oh, you big and bad now, right? Them speech contests gotchu all gassed up."

"And you ain't shit."

"Don't nobody want your sloppy seconds. Hoeing ass."

"I'm not the only one that sleeps in this house. I swear I will set your mangy ass on fire. You better hope Uncle Ross ain't got no gas in that can."

"Bitch."

"Your mama's a bitch and her mama, too."

I started carrying around a Zippo lighter. I sometimes flicked it at him as a warning, to remind him of what I'd do. I wasn't going to let anybody touch me like that again, the way that boy had in St. Ann, even if it meant burning the whole house down.

"You ain't gone do shit," he said one day.

I looked him in the eyes, clicked the spark wheel, and made a sizzling noise like the sound of chicken frying in grease.

"I can't do it," I said.

She waited me out, then said, "Try it again."

"It's too hard."

"That's why I gave it to you," she said.

We had a speech competition coming up and Mrs. LeCompte wanted me to use Finn's poem in the dramatic interpretation category. I hesitated, then demurred. She wouldn't take no for an answer.

In the first rehearsal session, I broke down during the delivery. Mrs. LeCompte taught me a visualization technique. I was to imagine something sad as if it were happening anew, she said.

"Stop, stop. Give it to me again. Give it to me."

The day of the contest, I stood in front of the classroom. A smattering of students—all of them white—looked on. The judge posted himself in the back.

"You may begin," he said, hitting the stopwatch.

I focused first on the pictures Auntie Killer took of Daddy in his coffin until I could see myself standing on the altar at Mercy Seat. And then, I thought back to the night Uncle Ross's grandson crawled on top of me and put his hand around my throat.

> *"It's the only thing that will assure me of what I cannot*
> *assure myself,*
> *that I'm really worthwhile, but I don't tell you this,*
> *I don't dare—"*

Between the shouts and whispers and tears, I was never more alive. The room was silent when I finished. I came home with first place in Dramatic Interpretation and Extemporaneous Public Address. The topic for the impromptu speech was the Iranian Hostage Crisis. The title was "444 Days in Tehran" and focused on the Algiers Accords.

During the awards ceremony, Mrs. LeCompte leaned over and said, "Where did you learn all of that?"

"Bernard Shaw. It was on CNN."

She smiled and shook her head.

There were more speech competitions, some in the district and some competing against other schools in the region. Soon, besting even the ninth-graders, I had a shoebox full of blue ribbons and medals. I found other poems, all of them speaking to me in different ways, but I kept coming back to Finn. Every line felt like it belonged to me and me alone. Finn had given me the voice I could not find in the church choir or even in the poems I had begun to write.

Auntie Gerald didn't like it. She said I sounded like an actress from one of her soap operas.

"Don't nobody wanna hear no salt wagon story," she said. "Ain't nothing special about sorrows. Everybody got'tum."

But I had found my voice, at least at school and in speech competitions, and I liked how it sounded. At home, when I wasn't locked in the bathroom working out the lines, I was largely silent. A tide of antipathy was still clear and present, but the fears were largely gone and I was becoming something new.

18

I was standing over the kitchen sink, scrubbing burnt chicken skin and grease out of a roasting pan when Auntie Gerald took me by the hand and led me up to her bedroom.

"Come on up and here and let me talk to you."

Going to her room always spelled trouble, but something was different. She hadn't growled my name as she typically did, so I wasn't sure what she wanted. Maybe it was the gentle way she cupped my fingers or the unusual softness in her voice. I remember how wonderfully she smelled, that night and always, being a woman who believed cleanliness was next to godliness. The old Babylonian proverb governed almost everything about her life, including the whistle-clean house we were forced to maintain.

She closed the door behind me and patted her bedspread, my cue to sit down. She studied my face, wrapped her meaty arm around my shoulders, and cast her eyes down to the shag carpeting.

"How you been feeling, Go Go? Mama said you threw up again this morning. You dizzy?"

"Sometimes, but I'm okay. My mama says she gets sick when her nerves are bad."

"When's the last time you came on your period?"

I thought for a moment and said, "I don't know."

"February, January?"

"No, ma'am."

"You sure? Think real good."

"Maybe Christmas."

"I need to carry you over to the clinic," she said, rubbing my thigh.

Auntie pulled her phone book out of her nightstand, flipping through the pages until she found the number. She checked her silver pearl-faced watch.

"They no doubt closed now. I'll call them tomorrow. Don't say nothing to nobody, you hear me?"

"Yes, ma'am. But, what's wrong with me?"

She teared up, looked me in the eyes, and said, "Ain't nothing wrong with you."

I immediately knew what she must have known. By her count, I hadn't had a period in two months, and I was likely pregnant. Auntie never did believe in asking questions she didn't want the answer to.

"Go take yourself a bath and get your bedclothes on."

"Yes, ma'am."

"Sleep upstairs with your grandmamma from now on, you hear?"

"Yes, ma'am."

"If somebody messes with you, you come tell me or Ross. I'ont care who it is. I'll knock the daylights out of them."

I nodded.

She lifted my chin and said, "You gone be alright."

Auntie wrapped her meaty arms around me, squeezing me into her bosom.

"Get you some rest, Go Go."

The next morning, I heard Auntie on the phone making the appointment. We'd be at the community health clinic all day, she said. Getting an appointment only meant the right to stand in line and get seen by a nurse at some point, which could take hours. The doctor didn't always show up.

The house was eerily quiet. Nobody traded good-mornings or even asked what the weather was like. Uncle Ross disappeared outside with a weedwhacker in his hand.

"Where you going, Ross?" Auntie Gerald called after him.

He said something about chopping down some weeds to clear the side field. He worked like that when something was on his mind.

I was pouring a bowl of Corn Flakes when the awkward silence broke as I yelped and I buckled over in pain, clutching my abdomen. I heard Grandma Alice screaming.

"Golleh!" she hollered. "Gerald! Come see 'bout Golleh."

Blood rushed down the back of my shorts. It felt like somebody was tightening a belt around my waist and jabbing my belly with a knife. I moaned like one of Uncle Ross's old hounds. Auntie reached the kitchen and sat me down. Grandma Alice fetched a bedsheet and called Uncle Ross in from the yard.

"We need to get her on over to St. Mary's," he said.

Uncle Ross wrapped me in the sheet and carried me out to the car. Auntie Gerald brought out a shirt for him to put on. The hospital was only a few blocks away. I lay in the back seat, watching the sky pass over our heads.

Hours later, after the doctor had come and gone, Auntie Gerald was allowed into the room. She hugged my head and kissed me on the cheek.

"It's gone be alright, Go Go."

Confused and scared, I asked, "Am I really pregnant?"

"You had a miscarriage."

"What's that?"

"It means you were pregnant, but the baby passed on."

Before I could drop a tear, Auntie Gerald said, "If the Good Lord wanted you to be a mother, you'd still be pregnant."

Faith was Auntie Gerald's answer to everything and, that day, it was mine. She took my hands into her palm and began to pray out loud.

"Heavenly Father, bless and protect this child. May she cleave unto you and find rest and comfort in your arms, Father," she started.

Her hands were soft like deep cushioned pillows over mine. Her voice, devoid of her usually hard tones, was soothing.

Back home, I overheard her talking to Grandma Alice.

"The doctor say she was about ten weeks."

"Did you call Mary Alice?"

"She don't need this heartache, Mama."

In the spring of '82, the school district put on a big parade. Along with my cousins and some neighborhood kids, we watched the Lincoln High School marching band and the majorettes, with their narrow waists and thick hips, decked out in black and orange, twirling down State Street. The girls' track team walked alongside a sleek slow-moving convertible, carrying the coach.

Coach Nino Fennoy and his Lincoln Lady Tigers had won the district championship again, after taking runner-up in the state meet the year before and winning it three straight years before that. Jackie Joyner was on the team back then and trained under Fennoy, along with Nicole Thompson, who was a year ahead of me at Rock. She later followed Joyner to UCLA on a full scholarship.

I'd tried and failed at various school sports and had been cut not once, but twice, from Coach Nave's track team. After managing to beg my way onto the squad, I joined the team for an endurance test at Parsons Field near Jones Park, which he'd set up after a particularly embarrassing track meet. We gathered around him and Mr. Parks, the unofficial assistant coach. Coach Parks was short and cross-eyed with a lopsided Afro as big as the moon.

"Give me two laps around that track," Coach Nave said, pointing to the cinder circle around us. "We aren't marking times, so take all day if you have to. Just finish."

A girl stuck her hand in the air.

"And what if we don't?"

"Don't what?"

"What if we don't finish, Coach?"

"Well," he said, looking up at the clouds. "Don't even wor'bout it."

"What does that mean?" another one said.

"It means don't worry about getting your cleats. Don't worry about when the bus is coming. Don't worry about showing up again. You cut. Turn in your uniform and don't even wor'bout it."

"Even the sprinters?"

"Don't even wor'bout it."

The first ten girls took to the line. Coach Parks blew the whistle and the group took off. Nicole led the pack before breaking away. When they finished, the next group stepped up. Parks blew the whistle again and they all finished with Toi Dixon coming in first.

I was in the third group, the "stragglers," as Coach Nave called us.

Again, Coach Parks blew the whistle.

I was out of breath after the third turn. By the time I started the second 440, my legs were wobbling and my chest was thumping like a set of bongos. Nauseous and dizzy, I stopped midway through the lap and walked the rest of the way. Four more sweaty-faced girls tailed in behind me.

Coach Nave met us at the finish line.

"Don't even wor'bout it," he said with a grin.

"But you didn't say run or walk," I said in protest. "You said finish even if it took us all day. We finished."

He could barely contain his laugh. The others waited, hopeful that he would see things my way, but I knew what was coming next.

"This ain't the debate team, Miss Lady," he laughed, "and I ain't Peggy LeCompte. This ain't no bookmobile."

I'd met the same fate earlier in the year when I went out for basketball. Coach Wren said I wasn't worth the cost of the extra uniform. Back in St. Ann, I was good enough to make starting point guard on the summer league team, hitting layups and hook shots like buttering bread. East St. Louis, where kids competed in AAU every summer and trained for junior high school squads like NBA players, was a different playing field. And, I didn't have the rhythm for a cheerleading squad that could've just as well subbed in for the Dallas Cowboy cheerleaders.

I was embarrassed. But two days later, after I couldn't finish the 880-yard run, the Iowa assessment scores came back.

Mrs. LeCompte laid the printouts on our desks. Scanning the percentiles, I grew sullen. My scores, marked with an X, were on one end of the scale, while the rest of the class either fell along the middle or on the opposite end. I thought I'd failed. I worried that they would call me stupid like Auntie Gerald and Bug did.

Mrs. LeCompte wandered the room, checking scores. I sheepishly handed her my printout.

"Wow," she said, her eyes bulging as she overenunciated the word. "Wow."

She took me out to the hall. The Iowa Test of Basic Skills

placed me between the ninety-eighth and ninety-ninth per-
centile in all ten sections, she explained.

"I'll make a copy for you to take home to your mother,"
she said.

"That's okay," I said, handing back the printout. "She
doesn't live with us."

"Who's been signing your report card?"

"My auntie," I lied.

Like the library card, I forged almost everything.

"Then, take it to her."

"Maybe she'll stop calling me Dum-Dum."

"Do you believe that?"

"Sometimes."

"Miss Taylor, you are a lot of things, but you aren't stupid. Never let anybody make you think that about yourself."

"Then why would they say that?"

"Sometimes hurt people try to hurt other people," she said.

It might've been that same day or another, but we got our
report cards. Mrs. LeCompte wrote the grade point average
ranking on the chalkboard. My name topped the chart. At
that point I hadn't yet earned a B since starting school. Word
about the Iowa scores and my grades got around. Coach Nave
gleefully started calling me Bookmobile.

I was sitting in the front row in class again. I never lost a
speech contest and, after two attempts, I'd finally made the
school performance choir. Mrs. Bolden spent hours at the
piano, running me through the scales, prodding me to hit the
notes. As it turned out, I wasn't tone-deaf after all. She had me
bend over and touch my toes, which forced me to sing from

my diaphragm. I was blue in the face and winded from repeatedly belting out the opening stanza of "The Star-Spangled
Banner" when she smiled and said, "First alto, Taylor."

Her approval unlocked something in me. I started singing
everywhere I went, again locking myself in Auntie Gerald's
bathroom to practice. She heard me once. I was hunched
over, blood rushing to my face, when she opened the door.

God sent His son.
They called him Jesus.
He came to love, heal, and forgive.
He lived and died to buy my pardon.
An empty grave is there to prove my Savior lives.

"You sound good," she said. "Keep at it. Make a joyful
noise unto the Lord."

I had done something that pleased her. It was decided then
that, if I maintained my grades, finished my chores, and kept
out of trouble, I could join in the school's traveling competition choir. By then, though, she started taking me almost
everywhere she went, rarely leaving me at home alone. From
the minute I was released from St. Mary's, something in her
changed. The rules and chores remained, but she spent more
time teaching me how to cook and sew. When Uncle Ross
brought home a new chessboard for me, she sat up late one
night letting me show her how to play. One morning, as I
dressed for school, I got up the nerve to ask her why she had
been so mean.

"I'm hard on you, because I know you gone do a lot of good in this world. Bring home anything less than a B and you'll be back to singing to that bathtub." Given that she'd only seen one report card, looking back, it was an empty threat. Even so, I understood her perfectly.

19

Mama started making it by Auntie Gerald's house more often. She'd been promoted to front desk manager, so she was no longer pulling late-night shifts. The hours and the pay got better, but there was something different about her.

I was coming in from school when I saw her burgundy Sunbird parked along the curb. I found her in the kitchen, sipping coffee with Grandma Alice. Auntie Gerald was standing over the stove starting dinner.

"How's school?"

"It's okay."

"I heard it's better than okay."

She wanted to see the medals I brought home from speech and debate contests. I went upstairs and got them from Grandma Alice's room. Auntie told her about "Invictus." Mama wanted to hear it. I looked at the ceiling and started rattling off the lines.

"You can say it better than that," Auntie Gerald said. "Show your mama how you do it."

"Yes, ma'am."

I closed my eyes, sucked in a breath, and started again.

> *"Out of the night that covers me,*
> *Black as the pit from pole to pole,*
> *I thank whatever gods may be*
> *For my unconquerable soul…"*

"That's so nice," Mama said. "You've always been so smart. What did she get on her report card, Gerald?"

"I ain't seen no report card, Mary Alice," Aunt Gerald piped in.

"I got all As."

When Auntie asked who signed it, I raised my brow and let out a sly grin. Mama did, too.

"Your father would be so proud of you," Mama said.

"I guess so."

"You guess? You was his Baby Girl. That's what he called you, you know?"

"I don't remember that."

The only real vision I had of Daddy was of his body in a coffin. I could vaguely remember the sound of his deep voice and, right then, I could count on one hand how many times I recalled seeing him. His life and his death remained largely a mystery to me. After he died, everybody kept whispering about how he was going straight to hell for everything he'd done. After a while, people stopped talking about him. It was as if he simply disappeared.

He was living with a woman named Urean when he was murdered. The house was around the way from the funeral home. I was with Mama when she stopped by. She told the woman that she could keep all the furniture. She was still his wife, she reminded the woman, and was entitled to everything he had. But she only wanted his gold lamp and a jewelry box decorated with metal lions.

"You want his bills, too, bitch?" Urean said.

We left to go pick out the casket. It was deep brown with bronze handles, and matched the suit Mama laid out for him.

Six days after he died, three white limousines rolled down Walter Street, bumping over potholes and spitting pebbles into the public housing complex. They took us across the river to Mercy Seat Baptist, where a throng of mourners filed into the pews for the memorial service. Grandma Alice had been a member there since the early 1940s, when the congregation numbered only a hundred or so.

It was early evening, just before dusk, when we entered the large brick church. We were surrounded by women in fur coats and fancy gloves and men wearing wide-brimmed fedoras with stately feathers tucked into their grosgrain hatbands. Grandma Cat followed my mother, my half brother, Christopher, and me into the majestic sanctuary. The choir stand was draped in velvet and the four pendant chandeliers glistened over the altar. For his funeral clothes, Mama chose a tailor-cut brown suit, a good tie and crisp cream dress shirt. The top of his head was slick bald, and his jet-black, shoulder-length hair flowed over a casket pillow encased in white silk. A bouquet of white roses and lilies adorned the coffin. I remember the shrieks and wails and shouting.

For all the money Mama plunked down for the elaborate memorial service, there wasn't any left for a headstone.

"Can you take me to see him?" I once asked.

She seemed confused at first.

"Out at Greenwood? Isn't that the name of his cemetery?"

She grew dewy-eyed and said, "Yes, it's Greenwood. Maybe next weekend when I'm off work."

The following Saturday came and went, as did the next and the next, until I asked Uncle Ross about it.

"Where is Greenwood Cemetery?"

"Over off Natural Bridge and Lucas and Hunt," he said. "It's up in St. Louis County."

"It is far away?"

"Closer than St. Ann."

"Then how come she won't take me?"

"It's still hard on your mama," he said.

I wouldn't let it go. I kept asking to go to Greenwood, until Uncle Ross told me he would talk to my mother about it. Tired of waiting, I left school one day and got on the Edgemont Bi-State bus. Riding across the bridge into St. Louis, I immediately regretted trying to go alone. The Natural Bridge bus route started downtown and went north through the city past Puckett's gas station. From there, according to the bus schedule, I was supposed to catch the Lucas and Hunt bus over to St. Louis Avenue.

The road map I stole out of Uncle Ross's glove compart-

ment said I had to walk three or four blocks down St. Louis
Avenue over to the cemetery.

I waited over an hour for the connecting bus to arrive. As
it happened, I was standing on the wrong corner waiting for
the Natural Bridge bus. It was getting on six o'clock before
an older lady in a nursing uniform next to me asked where
I was going.

"Out to Greenwood Cemetery," I said. "I'm supposed to
catch the Natural Bridge right here."

"Oh, child, that bus done come and gone. If you wait a
while, you can take the next King bus and get off at Lucas
and Hunt. It'll be dark before long."

I gave up and decided to go back. When I got home, the
sun was going down and the streetlights had begun to glow.
Living in East St. Louis, I had never been outside after dark
and the thought of it was terrifying. Auntie Gerald was standing on the porch.

"Goldie Taylor! Get'cho behind on up here! She out here,
Ross!"

Uncle Ross was sitting in the living room. He still had his
shoes on and his car keys in his hand.

"Your uncle been looking all over for you."

"I tried to go see my father."

"Out at Greenwood?"

"Yes, ma'am. I missed the Natural Bridge bus, so I came
back."

I don't think she knew what to say. Uncle Ross was quiet,
too. When I heard Grandma Alice call my name from upstairs, I sat on the steps and cried.

"Y'all oughta carry her on out there, Gerald," she said. "Ain't no reason to keep her from Wyart."

That Sunday after church, Auntie Gerald pulled Reverend Hubbard to the side for a quiet conversation. When we got home, instead of going to the kitchen to finish cooking dinner, she told me to change out my church clothes and get my Bible. Uncle Ross already had on his good slacks and a button-down shirt. He handed me a bundle of lilies tied up with a nice bow.

We got in the car. Magic 108 played gospel music on Sundays back then, but they stopped at noon and went back to R&B. Auntie settled for WESL, the weaker AM station where she could bob her head to the Mighty Clouds of Joy.

A groundskeeper stood in a small front office near the entrance. The cemetery otherwise was empty when Uncle Ross pulled along the gravel drive and stopped the car.

Marble markers dotted the lawn, some weathered and leaning. If Greenwood had been pretty once, it was hard to tell. The grass was neatly mowed, but there was no ornate stone gate, velvet-lined chapel or rows of well-trimmed shrubs.

From where we were standing, it was hard to believe there were so many graves. Uncle Ross pointed to the back.

"There's a lot more ground back there," he said.

"It's in Section A," Auntie Gerald said. "Over there, Ross."

Auntie walked us to the area, up near the main street, and pointed to an unmarked spot where my father had been laid to rest.

"I think it's right here, Ross."

"He was a good man," he said. "I sure do wish he could see you right now."

I stared down at the patch of grass.

"How come there isn't a tombstone?"

"He doesn't need one in heaven," Auntie assured me.

"I'ma go on back to the car," Uncle Ross said.

Uncle Ross, I knew, wasn't much for funerals and cemeteries.

Auntie grabbed my hand and started to pray out loud. When she was finished, she turned to me.

"Anything you wanna say?"

"I don't know."

"I wonder if he made it to heaven," I said. "I don't know what to say. I wish my daddy could hear me sing."

"Well, just sing something."

I stopped, look down at the patch of grass, and thought about it.

> *"Why should my heart feel lonely*
> *And long for heaven and home"*

Auntie brushed away her tears. I closed my eyes and kept going.

> *"His eye is on the sparrow*
> *And I know He watches me"*

When I was finished, she laid the lilies down.

"We'll see 'bout getting a tombstone," she said. "He deserve to have one."

When we returned home from the cemetery that Sunday, Grandma Alice called me into her room. She'd found a copy of my father's obituary tucked inside a family photo album. Flipping through the pictures, she pointed out familiar faces. She wouldn't say a bad word about him. Grandma Alice thought it better that I knew the good after hearing so much bad.

I wanted to know why people said he was going to hell. She would not answer, saying only, "He broke your mama's heart."

Candidly, there were moments when I did not want to know the truth about my father. There were things that I had romanticized, things wrapped in a sunny idealism of what it would've been like to have him present, protecting me from the ugliness, the mutilations and cruelties.

Even so, unlike my grandmother, I could not turn away from his terrors and how they complicated his relationship with my mother. Hers had been a fitful love that was informed, I believe, by her own traumas and marred by the pain of loving a man not quite capable of affording her the same fullness. Even if sometimes absent, my mother and I shared a connection to my father that bound us in specific and unique ways that my siblings, either for lack of blood or the inconveniences of street life, could never know. Even if he had saved my sister from torrential winds and rains, he was still the man who blacked my mother's eye and beat my brother with a doubled extension cord until Miss Hazel Byron stared him down and dared him to lay a hand on Donnie again.

I lay down in Grandma Alice's bed. I quietly wept. She patted my back like a baby until I drifted off to sleep.

BRILLIANT CORNERS

20

The first time I was raped, I lost my footing in the world, if indeed I'd ever had it. Then came the second attacks, by my own cousin. After the miscarriage, it was like somebody lit a fuse. I vacillated between rage and ambivalence. I forgot what joy felt like.

The burden of mothering me, an angry, disconnected, and rarely bathing girl who needed to be reminded about the virtues of soap and a toothbrush, fell on Auntie Gerald. Church, she knew, was the one thing that could soothe me. She picked out another solo song for me to sing.

Sometimes I feel like a motherless child
A long way from home,
A long way from home...

Back at home, there were hushed conversations about my schooling and whether I would fit in at East Side. My ninth-grade graduation from Rock wasn't far off, but I was fourteen going on fifteen. At least in Uncle Ross's mind, I wasn't old enough to catch the bus by myself. The senior high school was forty blocks away, up around Fiftieth and State Street, and I would have to take a Bi-State bus to get there every day. Given my track record with public transit, that made Uncle Ross uneasy.

"It ain't like it was when Michael was out there," he said, "I'll have to drive her back and forth every day."

"Your heart can't take all that. She'll be alright, Ross, as long as she don't come up pregnant again," Auntie Gerald said.

Auntie kept reminding me that extracurriculars were exactly that: extra. The privilege, like everything else, had to be earned. I was repeatedly put on punishment for one minor infraction after another. Coming in late from school late without a believable excuse meant more chores and losing whatever little freedom I had.

She found me wily and manipulative, I know, and for good reason. I spent most days scheming my way out of chores and concocting excuses to skirt the afternoon curfew.

"She knows how to work us," I heard Uncle Ross tell Auntie Gerald.

"She need to be right where I can see her," she said.

"We can't keep her locked up in the house," Uncle Ross said with a heavy sigh.

"I ain't saying that, Ross, and you know it."

He almost never argued with Auntie Gerald, and he wasn't about to start that day. Uncle Ross's job was to maintain the order his wife demanded, even if that meant taking a strap to our backsides. His affections were tied up in the belt he spanked us with.

I wasn't too old for a whipping, he reminded me. But my uncle, then in his midfifties, didn't have the strength he once had. He was frequently short of breath, complaining of chest pains, and was taking blood pressure medicine. The doctor gave him baby aspirin to ward off a stroke.

Bug said her son, Fat Man, had softened his ways. He was a good-natured rambunctious boy who had the run of the house. Bug was by then living with Joe Petty, a well-known drug lord, out in St. Louis County, and was pregnant again. So, it was up to Uncle Ross to make sure Fat Man was fed and saw him off.

He was sicker now, sicker than he'd ever been, popping nitroglycerin tablets to stave off the chest pains, and too tired to chase the little boy he loved more than pan-fried-bologna sandwiches. When he got winded, he'd grip his chest and ask somebody to get the bottle off his chest of drawers.

"Red," he'd whisper. "Go up there and get my medicine and get me some cold water."

The bouts of angina came closer together. Auntie, overweight with a heart condition and other maladies, was in failing health, too. Between the two of them, there was a minor pharmacy in their bedroom. Taking care of other people's children was a way of life and it wore them down.

This time, though, at least with me, there were more problems, good and bad, to work out. For all of their backwater ways, they knew I needed more schooling than I could get in East St. Louis. But I was finding my way. I'd won the race for student council president at Rock, which turned out to be more of an honor than an actual job, and Auntie told anybody who would listen and some who wouldn't.

"She used to call me Mama, you know? I dern near raised this child."

Though less frequently, she assured me my mother was coming back at some point. But Auntie Gerald was my mama in every meaningful way.

There were no real duties for student council, except that I was made Principal for the Day, sometimes read the morning announcements and was now enjoying some measure of regard from my classmates. Things got somewhat better after we won the district-wide Scholar Quiz Bowl.

My neighbor-cousin Claire and a boy named Cedric were both on the team. I'd beaten out Cedric in the student council race and just about everything else. It was him, though, who advanced to the last round. After a team huddle, it was decided that I would be the "ringer" and take his place. There was a loophole in the rules.

The contest was tied up. The last question was to name the president of Egypt. I hit my buzzer. The room got quiet.

"Mubarak," I said. "Hosni Mubarak."

Mrs. LeCompte was the faculty adviser. When it was over, she asked me how I knew the answer.

"You know they're going to say we cheated."

I'd heard it on the news when Israeli Defense Forces invaded Lebanon, I told her with a shrug.

"Operation Peace for Galilee," I said.

She eyed me with curiosity.

"What does PLO stand for?"

"Palestine Liberation Organization."

"And what do they want?"

"I don't really know."

That I had peculiar interests in English literature and esoteric equations, a near obsession with ghosts and ancient wars
and a father I could not have, was an added complication for
my aunt and uncle. Their responsibility, stated or otherwise,
was to see that I was fed and stayed out of trouble. That meant
more chores and church three times a week and other things
that kept me from getting caught up in the fires burning outside their front door. It had been a year since I blew up the
last Coke bottle in the backyard and I knew enough about
gravity not to climb out on the roof again. Unless I got into
a fight at school, which I sometimes did, they rarely got involved in academic matters.

"Red ain't the kind to let nobody push her around," Uncle
Ross said after one particularly ugly spat broke out after a basketball game in the spring of '83.

Patricia King, a tiny girl with a big mouth and a gang of
brothers, called me out my name. I never figured out why she
was mad at me and I didn't care. We were coming out of the
gym and walking through the gate when she shouted at me.

"What's up now, bitch! I heard you been talking about me
behind my back. Come on wit' it."

I paused, thought for a click, then turned around and sucker
punched her in the face.

Patricia had fists like Leon Spinks. Tired of taking her

licks, I dived in, headfirst, snatching her by the hair and rip-ping her white T-shirt in the process. We spilled out into the dark parking lot, cussing, and punching like a couple of wel-terweights in a prize match. Mr. McKnuckles tore us apart.

"Break it up and get on home!" he shouted.

"I know Bookmobile ain't out here fighting," Coach Nave said.

"She started it," Pat said, huffing and puffing.

"Coach, she called me the *b*-word," I said in my defense.

"Get on home, I said," McKnuckles growled again. "See me in the office Monday morning. Be there before the bell rings."

When I walked into the house that night, Grandma Alice noticed the scratches on my face and the red knot on my tem-ple. I looked like Achilles after he killed Hector. Pat, though, had found my proverbial heel. Whether out of disdain, jest, or affection, I hated being called out my name. And, if I thought I could do something about it, I would.

"Ross! Golleh been outdoors fighting."

I told him what happened.

"You can't go messing with them Kings," he said, dab-bing my cuts with peroxide-soaked cotton balls. "Y'ont know what they'll do."

"It's over with now," I said.

"It ain't never over for them Kings. Don't be out there fighting one of 'em by yourself."

"They start it, you end it," Auntie Gerald said.

"Make sure you ain't by yourself, Red," Uncle Ross said.

Other than his younger granddaughter, there weren't any

other Robinson kids at Rock and she was more prone to cut and run than ball up her fists.

"You think you can box the world." My cousin Peety giggled and said, "Look at you now."

"If she comes back, she's going to get it again," I said. "She better bring her brothers."

"How you gone be outside fighting when you still pissing in the bed?"

I felt my face get hot and reflexively curled my knuckles. Peety, who was twice my size, laughed and said, "You gone hit me now, too? That'll be the last swing you take."

21

"Who won?"

"It was a draw," Patricia said.

I smirked. "We can go again and settle it."

"Easy now, bruiser," McKnuckles said.

In the end, we got off light. Mr. Howell let me stay on the speech team and I wouldn't have to give up being student council president, but I had one more chance before he put me off the squad. Patricia was already pretty much the queen of in-school suspension and Mr. McKnuckles said she was working his "last nerve." He gave us both three swats and sent us on to class.

"Don't let me catch you after school, Bookmobile," Patricia said, passing me in the hallway.

"You got time, I got time."

Mrs. LeCompte thought I was strong enough to compete in speech and debate with both the junior and high school teams. I was in ninth grade then and still, technically, in junior high. She had a quiet conversation with the principal and the head coach out at East Side. They reviewed the rule books and agreed I was qualified.

"Does that mean I'll be going up against seniors?"

The choice was not mine, but it would mean traveling around the state with both teams and, thus, more time out of the house. I wouldn't be there to fetch Uncle Ross's medicine when he got sick, but it also meant less trash to burn and fewer pots to scrub.

"If y'ont use your gifts, God'll giv'um to somebody else," Grandma Alice frequently reminded me.

Auntie didn't like the idea that I would be around older students. She bought me a new skirt and a crisp white blouse for performances, which doubled as church clothes, and said if I ever ran into trouble, I should call home collect. I was both nervous and excited, although neither would last.

Mrs. LeCompte said I was more than ready and that she also planned to submit my writing to upper-level essay contests. Another student from Hughes-Quinn Junior High School, the daughter of a substitute teacher, was also elevated. Together, we crisscrossed Illinois from Madison to Peoria to Chicago and nearly every point between. Most often, we took first and second place, beating out our high school teammates.

McKnuckles said I was a bone collector.

I had begun performing a piece called "Please God, I'm Only 17." The essay was originally published in an Ann Landers column and, not infrequently, someone wrote the newspaper asking her to run it again. The voice was a boy who was killed in a drunk driving accident.

"The day I died was an ordinary school day," it started. "How I wish I had taken the bus."

I'd found the essay in the *St. Louis Post-Dispatch* and first performed it for that year's Optimist Club contest. By the time I finished, my face was soaked.

"Please don't put me in the ground. I promise if you give me one more chance, God, I'll be the most careful driver in the whole world. All I want is one more chance!"

The state speech contest was held in Peoria at Bradley University that year and we were the only Black team at the event. The rehearsals had been rigorous. We trained in the high school auditorium. While my teammates performed passages from famous Black authors, I wrote an original essay. It wasn't a good idea, the high school coach lamented, but Mrs. LeCompte was unmoved. I'd written about Father Moses Dickson. My paternal grandfather, Wyart Sr., was buried in a colored cemetery that bore his name.

At its founding, Father Dickson Cemetery was formally dedicated by the Knights of Tabor and Daughter of the Tabernacle. Moses Dickson was born a free man in Ohio in 1824. He was a leader in the Underground Railroad and an ordained minister in the African Methodist Episcopal Church. Together with twelve other men, he went to St. Louis to work out a covert, violent plan to end slavery. They published a book that outlined their group's constitution, as well as the governing rules and regulations. They called themselves the

Knights of Liberty and my grandfather was a descendant of one of the militiamen.

On competition day, we boarded a yellow school bus for the trip up I-55. Once there, we separated into classrooms as the judges took their seats. Talking about abolitionists was a gamble. It had been enough to win the first round of the state speech contest but, during the lunch break, Mrs. LeCompte wondered if I might be better off reciting Finn's poem "Please Hear What I'm Not Saying."

I hesitantly agreed.

"You need to bring the house down," she said. "They don't think you belong here, but you earned this."

I walked into the crowded lecture hall, steadied myself, and waited for my name to be called. There were so many faces, all older than me, and I felt small. Rising from my chair, I thought back to my father's funeral and the obituary Grandma Alice gave me. In that moment, the rows of white people disappeared and I was alone with myself.

Sometimes shouting and sometimes in nonchalant even tones, I had a sureness about me. I looked directly at the center judge. I was crying now, but I was keeping my pace. And so was the judge. After another break, we reconvened in a large theater hall for the awards ceremony. Sitting on the end of a row near the center of the room, Mrs. LeCompte gripped my hand as the winners were announced. Finally, the moderator started to call my category. After losing third and second place, I figured it was over.

"And first place in Dramatic Interpretation goes to Goldie Taylor from East St. Louis Senior High School!"

It was a shocking outcome, for me and everyone else. I thought it was a mistake and didn't get up until Mrs. LeCompte nudged me. I walked up to the stage to receive the trophy. After the initial spate of applause, murmurs broke out in one section of the audience. We soon learned that a faculty adviser from another team would challenge the judging and whether or not I was qualified to compete. I wasn't even supposed to be there, they said, and I hadn't given the same speech during all the rounds. They wanted me to give the trophy back.

Mrs. LeCompte refused. The rule books stated clearly that the competition was open to ninth to twelfth graders from any public school in the state of Illinois and I had won qualifying rounds at the district and regional level. The other schools knew I was coming and they knew my reputation, she said.

After the earlier events, the local newspaper had run announcements with photographs of the winners. Auntie Gerald had proudly collected the clippings and put them in the family photo album. She'd even made a big announcement at church and Mrs. LeCompte wrote about it in her weekly column in the *Monitor*.

On the second point, the East Side coach demanded that the contest organizers show him the guidelines forbidding original essays or banning a change in performance pieces between rounds. It was resolved that I'd won fair and square.

As we exited the building, heading back to the bus, a white kid, a boy I beat, walked up, and spit at me. He missed. I hauled back to take a swing. A teammate, a junior I think, grabbed me by the waist and tugged me away.

"Keep going," he said, pulling me. "They're just mad because we came up here and whipped them in front of their own people."

The boy laughed as we walked away.

We loaded onto the bus and listened as Mrs. LeCompte gave us a lecture on winning with grace. After the commotion about my qualifications and what that boy had done, I didn't want to act like I didn't care. Had it been the high school football or track squads, rather than the more studious speech team, I thought to myself, it might not've ended until the police showed up.

Auntie Gerald chided me for letting somebody get under my skin like that. She agreed with Uncle Ross's house rules when it came to scuffles: one fights, we all fight. But that did not apply to knocking a white boy on his ass so far away from home.

"People like that will use what little power they got to turn the whole system on you," she said.

Uncle Ross disagreed. He looked at me severely and said, "You should've cleaned his clock."

22

The days were gone when I had to squirrel away overdue library books in the bottom of my grandmother's chifforobe. I had a new diary. While I used to chronicle the maltreatment, the lack of food and absence of compassion, the pages were now filled with dreamy passages about a boy I liked.

Brian was a junior at East Side and we were both on the speech team. A tennis player, he was caught up in sports and pretty girls, girls who weren't stroppy bookworms with bad acne and buckteeth and believed in the basic value of soap and warm water. For all of the progress I'd made on other fronts, Uncle Ross still had a hard time getting me to put on deodorant with any regularity. I'd never had good hygiene, if only because there had been nobody around to press the issue as I came of age. Try as he might to convince me otherwise, I didn't see the point. And, although less frequently,

I was still scrubbing the urine out of the living room carpet when I slept.

While they had at one time teased me over my predilection for reading *World Book* encyclopedias and *Childcraft* books from cover to cover, and belittled me for "acting" and "talking white," my older cousins now focused on my hygiene deficiencies. Auntie Gerald's son Michael routinely called me Dirty Red.

"Call that little Darnell over here," Bug would tease. "That'll get her in the bathtub real quick."

She wasn't wrong about that.

I was far away from St. Ann, both in body and spirit. I missed Mrs. Farrell's lopsided birthday cakes with green food coloring and trips to the Northwest Plaza with Debbie to shop at Spencer's gift shop. I missed having neighbors like Mr. Altepeter, even if he didn't speak to us, and I wanted a nice dog like Chip rather than the mutts tied to Uncle Ross's tree. There were plenty of bad things about our old neighborhood, but it wasn't an open-air drug market, kids my age weren't getting shot, and we didn't go to school in a rundown building. Yet East St. Louis had given me something that would have been impossible to experience in St. Ann.

Here, in our wounded and struggling city, Black was beautiful, even if it sometimes needed to be shined and re-stitched like an old pair of shoes. When a fire broke out in the main building of our school, sending us all rushing out onto the street, I thought for sure the district would knock it down and build another. But days later the mess was largely cleaned up, the scorches and scars brushed over. We went back to class in rooms with fresh coats of latex paint, but the smell of smoke still lingered.

Amid the proliferation of crack cocaine and the destruction it wrought, we were told that with enough hard work, with enough discipline and grace, we could achieve anything.

"Be excellent in all that you do," Mrs. LeCompte reminded us. "Be so good that your gifts cannot be denied."

There was both a magnificence and an irony in that. We measured ourselves by what Toni Morrison called the "white gaze." If we dressed and comported ourselves in a manner deserving of respect then we would receive it. No one mentioned that Medgar Evers had been wearing nice slacks and a tie the day he was shot down in his driveway. Nor did anybody mention that women were often lynched in their church stockings and good dresses. Be dutiful, they said, and no one will question your place. But mine had been questioned repeatedly. The challenges started coming even before competition day. Auntie Gerald told me to "keep giving it to them."

"You every bit as good as any one of them dern white kids from them fancy schools," she said. "You good because you work on it. You keep working, you keep giving it to them."

In late spring of '83, I was invited to join the high school squad in Chicago. There was another speech contest at the University of Illinois–Chicago Circle. I took first place that day, beating out Brian and another junior high school girl from Hughes-Quinn. The daughter of one of our substitutes, she was something of a savant. She was pretty, always wore nice clothes, and had the grace I couldn't muster. After the awards ceremony, the team went to city hall for a brief meeting with Mayor Harold Washington.

He leaned back deep in his chair, admiring our team, and told us all how proud he was. He'd visited East St. Louis the prior year and Auntie Gerald, an election precinct captain, was on the welcoming committee. I'd remembered seeing him address the rally and told him so. I explained how I'd convinced Principal Howell, using Title IX, to get into the all-boys shop class instead of home economics. I prattled on, talking at lightning speed, until one of our faculty advisers stopped me.

She told him what I had done that year.

"And she's only in ninth grade."

"Is that so?"

"Yes, sir."

He likened me to a bag of lit firecrackers.

"You're something special," he said, laughing. "And you sure do talk a lot!"

In 1983, Eddie Murphy was in his third season on *Saturday Night Live*. I didn't have to sneak downstairs to listen to Uncle Ross's Richard Pryor records or beg Grandma Alice to let me watch Johnny Carson. I was around seven when Mama put me out of the room when Pryor and Chevy Chase performed their classic "Racist Word Association Interview."

At fourteen, Auntie said I was old enough to watch *SNL*. I'd been allowed to watch the Christmas show in '82, when Murphy hosted and did a Gumby sketch. Auntie Gerald bought me a new tape recorder to replace the one Ronnie Lee stole out of our house. She packed the box with batteries, a sleeve of blank cassettes and two new gospel recordings from the Clark Sisters and the Winans.

Murphy was young, Black, and funny. My cousins Bug and Carol Brown fantasized about meeting him.

"Just give me one night!" Bug exclaimed.

I would've given anything to go to New York and sit in the audience. Every Saturday, I popped popcorn in Grandma Alice's cast iron skillet to watch the show. I was getting older, but I still wasn't allowed to go to school parties and sleepovers were forbidden. I didn't mind being stuck at home with Eddie Murphy. I didn't know how to dance anyway, at least not like Bug and Lori Ann. While Grandmaster Flash and the Furious Five was on the radio and kids were break-dancing in the street, I had the rhythm of Robot B-9 from *Lost in Space*.

At home, the once petty thievery now felt like an all-out assault. Anything of value that wasn't locked up, bolted down or too heavy to carry out the door went missing. Auntie Gerald knew it had to be Ronnie Lee. She wouldn't cut him loose, but she was no fool.

One night, I heard her yelling at him up in her bedroom.

"If you'll steal from your own mama, you'll steal from anybody!"

"Mama, I ain't took nothing out of here."

"Hand me my house key," she said. "You can knock on the door."

"What if ain't nobody here?"

"Then you ain't gone be here, either."

Ronnie's problems, like my brother's, were only just beginning. He was hopped up on something and Auntie suspected it was more than marijuana. I remember the first time I heard the word *crackhead.*

By the early eighties, crack cocaine was starting to make its way across the Midwest. Produced by cooking cocaine powder and baking soda, it was dirt cheap. Highly addictive, the crystallized rocks devastated all eighty-nine blocks of East St. Louis. It left few families unscathed, including ours.

Late that March, the entire ninth grade got on school buses for a day trip to Six Flags Over Mid-America. Uncle Ross bought my ticket. Grandma Alice packed a sack lunch and gave me ten dollars to spend. I called Puckett and he told Auntie Gerald that he would pay her back if she gave me another ten dollars. I got on the bus and sat near the back to sneak a listen to Deborah's Walkman radio. I was trying to memorize the words to a new rap song when a bus monitor confiscated the device.

"You can have it when we get back."

We were all wearing matching purple-and-white T-shirts and the trip was supposed to celebrate our upcoming graduation from junior high school. Told to meet back at the bus at 4:00 p.m., we flooded into the theme park. By early afternoon, Deborah convinced me to get on the Screamin' Eagle roller coaster. After the terrifying ride, we were descending the stairs when I spotted an attendant who was leaving his shift. I saw him looking back and blushed.

"He's looking at you!" Deborah said.

"For real?"

"For real, girl, he's looking at you!"

For at least the next hour, dipping in and out of crowds, we tailed him around the park grounds. We waited while he went into a back area and came out wearing white shorts and a striped polo shirt. He smiled at us and kept walking.

"You should go talk to him," Deborah prodded.

"Nuh-un," I said.

"So, we just gone follow him around all day?"

At one point, near the front gate, he stopped suddenly and turned around.

"Hi."

"Um, hi," I said.

"Are you following me?"

"No, why would you think that?"

He smiled.

"I'm Kenneth."

Deborah elbowed me in the side.

I was mesmerized by the way the corner of his mouth curled up when he smiled, his cocoa brown skin and the slight rasp in his voice. He was older than us, I knew, because the fuzz on his upper lip was filling in. His soft brown eyes lit up in the sun.

"Um, I'm Goldie."

"That's a pretty name. Hey, how old are you?"

"I'm sixteen," I lied, figuring he was probably in high school. "I go to East Side."

"The football team is really good."

"Yeah, they are. Where do you go?"

"I'm at Mizzou."

I had no idea what or where that was, but I pretended I did.

"I have to drive back tomorrow. Say, can I call you?"

"Sure."

"So, you will have to give me your number."

Deborah, who always had a pen tucked behind her ear, gleefully handed it over.

"I don't have any paper," he said.

"Here, I'll write it on your hand."

He watched me as I scribbled it out.

"Open your hand. I'll give you mine. I have two. One at school and one at home."

A wave of confusion washed over my face.

"Oh, Mizzou is in Columbia. It's about two hours away. My house is down in the city. My parents live off Goodfellow."

"My godfather's gas station is close, I think. It's on Kings-highway and Natural Bridge."

"Mr. Puckett is your godfather? I get gas there all the time."

As it turned out, Kenny was finishing his freshman year at University of Missouri–Columbia. He was nineteen years old. I suppose he hadn't noticed that the name of our junior high school was emblazoned on the back of my purple T-shirt that day at Six Flags, but it didn't take long for the lie to unravel.

I invited him to come over two weeks later. He got there that night as Auntie Gerald and Uncle Ross were about to leave for another Elks Lodge party down at the Regal Room. His beat-up old blue Pinto came rumbling down the street, passing our house, right as my uncle was backing out of the driveway.

Peety and I shouted out his name. Kenneth stopped his car and backed up the one-way street.

"Park over there," Peety said, pointing across the street. "Girl, he's so fine," she said, turning to me.

Peety helped me sneak him into the house. He was shorter than I'd remembered, around my brother Donnie's height, which I thought was perfect. I thought everything about him was perfect.

He didn't know he wasn't supposed to be there and it wasn't long before Bug busted us in the basement. The lights were on and so were our clothes, but Bug took one look at Kenneth and wasn't satisfied.

"What'chall doing down here and who is you?"

"Kenneth."

"Kenneth what?"

"Kenneth Goins."

"And how old are you, Kenneth Goins?"

"I'm nineteen."

"Do you know how old she is?"

Kenneth looked at the floor.

"I told him I was sixteen," I muttered.

"Girl, you gone get this boy put in jail. Tell him how old you are, for real."

The fact that I was only fourteen, turning fifteen that summer, hit him like a ton of bricks, he'd later say.

Bug never told on us, but Kenneth called less often after that. Although, he still did. The conversations were brief and friendly, and he admitted that he'd been following us, too. While he had no idea what I was going through at home, Kenneth helped me make sense of the world I was living in. He talked about the politics of race and poverty in stark terms.

Peety called it "puppy love," only I didn't feel like a puppy. On some level, though, it was very much love. Kenneth was pulling me along both emotionally and intellectually in ways a boy my own age never could. He steadfastly refused to cross the line, and that made it a safe space. Kenneth was all at once the brother I never truly had, the teacher I craved and the friend I needed most. It wasn't what I wanted, but it had to be enough.

23

Mama left L.C.

One Saturday, she drove up to Auntie's house without stated cause or notice. She came toting an armload of clothes, boxes of shoes and other personal effects. Mama didn't have any furniture, and no curtains, no sheets, or bedspreads. Everything in the St. Ann house she'd sold off to salvage when she set up house with L.C. She figured, I guess, that it would last forever. But, somewhere along the line, things broke down, spewing vapors like an old radiator.

At least in the beginning, he'd meant the world to her and her to him. That much I know. I also know there had been other women and other transgressions she didn't have the words to explain. For my part, I'd only seen them when they were in love, cooing at each other like two stout-bodied pigeons.

"Is she white?" I heard Auntie Killer ask her one time.

"I couldn't tell you, Doris Jean. I just know it ain't none of me."

L.C. had been married twice before, one of them, the last, was a white lady who now lived in Texas with their two boys. The first was Black, and the mother of his oldest daughters, two tall lanky women who looked just like their daddy with a wide, deep dipping philtrum, strong cleft chins, and bulb eyes that sat back in their sockets like cue balls. My mama was supposed to be his third and last wife. I wondered then why anybody would really want to be anybody's third anything.

L.C. liked to be taken care of, my mother would say, and she didn't mind. She'd been raised that way, to cater to a man's needs and let him have the run of his kingdom.

"Every man needs a throne," Grandma Alice would say.

Mama pushed the idea of getting married until L.C. got tired of hearing about it. He was running out of excuses, apparently, when he caved and asked her to move in with him. It was a trial run. He was kicking my mother's tires.

"Why would any man buy the dern cow when he got the milk for free?" Auntie Gerald said.

They talked like that when Mama was out of earshot. There were mutual jealousies. Auntie had a husband, who'd bought her a house and saw after her worldly needs and, in her mind, my mama was living the high life afforded by a fancy job and men who wouldn't do her right for more than a few minutes at a time. Auntie was heavyset, and well put together. Mama sometimes bought dresses at Neiman-Marcus out at Frontenac Plaza off Lindbergh. They got on like that, helping one another out of various ruts and grumbling about what the other one had and the other one didn't.

Still, there was no thicker love.

Uncle Ross helped Mama get situated in Michael's old bedroom next to Grandma Alice. He installed a padlock and helped her assemble a clothes rack where she hung her dresses.

I had not seen or heard from my mother in a few months, and I was surprised that Saturday morning when she turned up with her car packed to the gills. But what I remember most from that time is how she was sad. Despondent and given to sporadic soft tears, she talked with pregnant sighs. Mama drank more heavily than I'd remembered and often came home drunk after work in the evening.

We slept together on a roll-out sofa bed that took up most of the upper bedroom. The mattress was thin and lumpy. You could feel the metal trundle frame underneath. But Mama kept it pulled out and made up with one of Grandma Alice's pretty blankets. I sometimes heard her weeping in the night and I remember the sickly sweet smell of liquor as she snored.

I assumed it was temporary and that she'd be leaving again at some point. Auntie was still doing the mothering, while my mother gathered what remained of her life in the small bedroom with cracked walls and chipped paint that overlooked the lower back roofline.

"Pride goeth before the fall," she said, folding her laundry one day.

She'd given over the independence she'd fashioned for herself to a man who traded her in like a used car. At forty-two, she had a good job but no place to call her own. The floor-model console television she worked so hard to pay off was gone now, too. She'd given up everything and left with next to nothing.

Over the previous two years, from the start of summer in 1981 until she came back in late spring of '83, I tried to become the color of water, translucent and fading into the background. Surviving meant making myself small, to be present yet unnoticeable and as uncatchable as air. Now, though, life was different. I wasn't exactly popular, but I had friends and I was class president. I was enjoying school as much as such a thing could be enjoyed at Rock. And, since I'd threatened to light him on fire in his sleep and Kenneth started coming around, Uncle Ross's grandson had mostly left me alone.

With my mother gone and living with a man I had come to despise like the Jell-O salad molds cousin Dot Brown used to bring over on bridge club nights, in time, I'd mostly picked up my own pieces. I was resentful now, Auntie Gerald knew.

"She still your mama," she reminded me.

Auntie Gerald, for better or worse, had filled in the voids. She warned me against being spiteful.

"She always gone do what she need to do to take care of you."

Bug was living off and on in the basement then. She was dating a man a decade or more older named Joe Petty. He was younger than my mother, but they knew one another from the nightclub scene in St. Louis. It was impossible, I later learned, not to know who Joe Petty was. His name often popped up in the newspapers, although I did not immediately make the connection. He knew the Slays and other important people in town. Bug spent most of her time at his place on Sacramento out in Northwoods.

Bug, though, didn't like that Mama had moved in. I overheard her one night on the phone in the basement.

"Auntie brought her little boxes in here," she told Ronnie Lee's ex-girlfriend Gloria, "and now we got bugs, Glo. It's roaches in the kitchen."

I ran upstairs to tell my mother, who was getting dressed for work. Mama stomped to the basement and stuck her finger in Bug's face, cussing so loud that Auntie heard her two floors up.

"What's going on down there?" she yelled from the top of the basement steps.

"Goldie lying! She lying on me, Auntie Mary Alice! I ain't say nothing about you, Auntie, I swear."

I'd never seen Bug scared before. She cut her dewy eyes at me. I was scared, too, scared she was going to tell my mother about my fledgling friendship with Kenneth.

"What exactly did she say?" Mama asked.

"She said there were roaches in your boxes when you moved in and now the house is infested."

"We ain't got no dern roaches!" Auntie shouted. "Goldie Taylor, I done told you about your dern mouth."

"I didn't say infested," Bug snapped back with an unwitting confession.

My mother caught on immediately.

"Call Glo back. I wanna talk to her myself," Mama said. Bug didn't move.

"What she need to call Glo for, Mary Alice?" Auntie asked.

Bug got up to leave the room. Mama stepped between her and the stairs.

"I said pick up that phone, goddammit! If you ain't say it, then Glo can prove it!"

Bug retrieved the handset and dialed. Sniffing out what was happening, Gloria covered for her. Mama knew it was a lie.

"Me and my boxes will be gone soon enough," she said.

24

I tried calling Kenneth at his dorm and then at his mother's house. His younger brother Steven picked up and politely told me he was talking on the other line.

"I'll tell him you called."

Later, I was washing dishes, soaking my hands and my feelings in the sudsy water, when the phone on the kitchen wall rang.

"Hey," he said, "what's up?"

"How did you know it was me?"

"I know your voice," he said.

"I know yours, too."

"I'm at home this weekend. If you're not busy, I could come over."

"Over here?"

"Your parents would need to be there. I can't sneak in your house again."

"You want to meet my mother?"

"Is she nice?"

"Kind of. When she's here. She works a lot."

I still hadn't told Mama about Kenneth. Uncle Ross picked up the phone once, but he assumed he was just another boy from school that he had to tell I couldn't have phone calls after eight o'clock.

"Who calling here after you?" Auntie Gerald asked.

"His name is Kenny," I said.

"Well, tell this Kenny you can't have calls after eight."

After some pleading and some measured sighs, my uncle gave me permission to visit with Kenneth, but only when he was home.

I spent all afternoon getting ready. For once, nobody had to remind me to bathe and put on good clothes. I picked out a sundress and some sandals and asked Peety to press out and curl my hair.

Mama wasn't there when Kenneth drove up. Uncle Ross offered to check his engine, on account of the knocking noise, but he politely declined.

We sat on the porch and waited for my mother. It was getting dark.

"She got off work at six, I think. She should be here by now."

"Did you tell her I was coming?"

"My uncle did."

"Oh, that's your uncle. I thought he was your father."

"My father died when I was five."

"What happened? I mean we don't have to talk about it if you don't want to."

"It's okay. He was murdered. Uncle Ross is pretty much my daddy."

"I'm sorry that happened to you."

He wrapped his arm around me and let my head fall into the cup of his shoulder. We stayed out on the porch swing, talking to the stars. I explained the situation, leaving out the bad parts. I could not bring myself to tell him that I had been raped by my cousin, or that I'd been pregnant and miscarried. I am sure he could smell the trauma wafting off my bones.

"My mother and my aunt are really close, too," he said. "Anyway, if we're going to be friends, I think I should meet her."

"I guess so."

"You know I'm in college, right?"

"Yeah."

"So, that means I really can't be your boyfriend."

"I know."

"I like you," he said. "You're cute and you're smart. I think it's cool that you're only fourteen and you like James Baldwin."

"I'm fourteen and a half. And doesn't everybody?"

"No," he said, laughing, "and not everybody is as cute and smart as you."

"But not cute and smart enough to be your girlfriend."

"You're not old enough to be my girlfriend."

I wouldn't let myself cry. I stared off into nothing and said, "'Ritie, don't worry 'cause you ain't pretty. Plenty pretty women I seen digging ditches or worse. You smart. I swear to God, I rather you have a good mind than a cute behind.'"

"Maya Angelou?"

I told Kenneth about the test scores and all the speech competitions that night and he asked where I wanted to go to college. I hadn't thought about it much, I told him.

"There's this school called Princeton that I read about," I said.

"You would move all the way to New Jersey?"

"I don't care where I go. I just want to leave here. I ain't never coming back."

He brushed my cheek and kissed my forehead.

"I am never," he said, correcting me, "and never let where you are become who you are." He got up to leave. "Say, if I write you a letter, will you write me back?"

"I guess so."

I did cry that night. There had at last been a boy, a young man really, too many years older and too far away, but somebody whose affections were worth having. His letters came every few weeks and, as promised, I wrote back. When Kenneth called, Uncle Ross would make him hang on until he tracked me down. Uncle Ross saw him as a positive influence, I imagine, and for once Auntie Gerald did not veto the idea.

When Kenneth asked me out for pizza, Mama decided it was time to meet the young man in question and told him to come into the house. She was putting on her makeup and getting ready for work when he got there. She summoned him into Auntie's upper bedroom. Their conversation didn't last long, but Kenneth came out sweating if not somewhat amused.

"What did she say?"

"She said I could take you to dinner. Are you ready?"

"Do I look okay?"

"You always do."

I peppered him with questions the whole way to Godfather's Pizza. I wanted him to hold my hand, like Mama and L.C. did when they were driving. He didn't.

He wouldn't tell me everything my mother said, but he let on that she'd issued a warning.

"If my daughter comes up pregnant, I'm coming to your door."

There was no chance of that, but Kenneth admitted that he found her frightening.

"You said she was nice."

"I said kind of. She probably just wanted to scare you."

"She did."

"Does that mean you're never going to kiss me?"

"I already did."

"You know what I mean."

"I'd rather you have a good mind than a cute behind."

Reverend Jesse Jackson came to town that year. The district convened a joint assembly attended by both public high schools and two junior highs. Uncle Ross's grandson and I were two of the students he plucked from the crowd in the auditorium, one as a standout student and the other an athlete. I was standing in the rafters and my cousin was lined up with the Lincoln High School choir. Jackson questioned us both about how we spent our afterschool hours.

When Reverend Jackson asked his name, I wanted to shout out, "Rapist!" There were at least five hundred students in that auditorium, and I wanted to tell them all what my cousin had done to me.

At the time, I assumed Jackson was unaware that we were related when he publicly chastised my cousin for putting more than twenty hours a week to organized basketball and track and nearly none toward his studies. The pastor rattled off the stats, pointing out the unlikelihood that anyone sitting in the gym would ever set foot in an NBA locker room. One minute he was bragging about his athletic prowess. In the next, my cousin was visibly embarrassed.

Jackson then launched into a soaring speech about academic excellence.

"Push! Excel!" he called out.

He told us to repeat after him.

"If my mind can conceive it!"

"If my mind can conceive it!"

"And my heart can believe it!"

"And my heart can believe it!"

"I can achieve it!"

"I can achieve it!"

For me, loving Black people, particularly my own family, had come at an extraordinary personal cost and some of the resentments were still there, charred and smoldering like my old diary on the trash pile. Balancing those feelings against the love I needed to believe was present, if never spoken, weighed on me. It was Maya Angelou's *I Know Why the Caged Bird Sings*, and the ways in which her life mirrored mine in so many ways, that helped me reckon with the dysfunction and the existential threat of coming of age in a place like East St. Louis. For me, this was my Stamps, Arkansas.

"The Black female is assaulted in her tender years by all those common forces of nature at the same time that she is caught in the tripartite crossfire of masculine prejudice, white illogical hate and Black lack of power," Angelou wrote.

"The fact that the adult American Negro female emerges a formidable character is often met with amazement, distaste and even belligerence. It is seldom accepted as an inevitable outcome of the struggle won by survivors and deserves respect if not enthusiastic acceptance."

I knew the women in my family to be survivors. The multiplicity of assaults and traumas and confusions were as common among them as spilled table salt and splattered bacon grease. I had not escaped that lot. That we were alive, even if eking out a menial existence, was something, I thought. It wasn't everything I wanted, but it was something, even if it stung.

And now I had Baldwin, Angelou, Walker and, to some extent, the words of Brother Malcolm, dictated in Haley's prose. In his autobiography, I came upon a single, haunting line: "It is only after slavery and prison that the sweetest appreciation of freedom can come."

My world was bigger with Kenneth in it. My goings and comings with him, while still rare, were liberating. While I was focused on schoolwork and winning competitions, I was consumed by Black literature, largely of the classic and socially antagonistic sort, and Kenneth helped me ventilate the ideas I encountered. "There is a heaviness in knowing that the blind will never need carry," I wrote in one essay. I had not escaped the distaste and belligerence Angelou wrote about. Like Uncle Ross's trash pit, it burned more furiously by the day. Only now, I spent that bitter energy on speech competitions.

During a final school event that year, I recited Walker's "For My People." Kenneth came to the academic awards banquet. He stood next to the auditorium door as I took to the center court. I was nervous.

And then, in my head, the room disappeared. My voice moved like a sermon, traveling rapid-fire through some lines, and sauntered like a cruise ship through others.

If I remember correctly, there had been a weeks-long teacher's strike and we had only been back in school a few days before the assembly. As the contract negotiations heated up, at Mrs. LeCompte's behest, I'd written a column for the *Monitor* newspaper urging the sides to work it out so we could return to the classroom. It had started as an essay that I mailed to her house in Belleville. Mama snipped it out and put in the family photo album along with the other clippings Auntie had collected. Mrs. Caradine, the loan shark's wife, summoned me across the street to tell me how proud she was of me.

"You keep on telling it like it is," she said. "Don't let nobody shut you up."

She made it clear that it wasn't a license to talk back to

grown folks, as I was becoming more and more prone to do. "Pick your battles," she admonished.

It was her idea to form a picket line.

I rounded up several of my school friends, made posters and marched in front of the District 189 offices. Before I left the house that day, I called a local news station. They sent a reporter out to interview me. I didn't know anything about the contract negotiations, I explained on camera.

"We belong in school," I said. "Some of the kids don't have anything else to eat all day."

Uncle Ross made everybody gather in the living room and watch it on television. When it was over, Auntie Gerald scolded me for getting too big for my britches. "The world will be there when you get there," she said.

There would be more essays and more fights to wage, but now, I was using something other than my fists.

"Keep it up, Red, and you gone wind up in that history book," Uncle Ross said with a grin.

Kenneth's mother, a schoolteacher, saw the story, too. She was proud of me, she said, but she also had something to say about my friendship with her son.

"There's a big difference between fourteen and nineteen," Mrs. Goins said. "Years from now, when you're twenty-four and he's twenty-nine, or even when it's the difference between thirty-four and thirty-nine, it won't mean a thing."

I told her I understood, but that he was important to me and that I had few people I could talk to.

"If you ever need someone to listen, I am always here," she said.

When she wasn't dealing with her own seven children, who ranged from early teens to adults, I talked to Mrs. Goins with some regularity. Kenneth's father, Wendell, sometimes answered.

"Which one you want to talk to?" he'd say.

After my ninth-grade graduation, sometime that summer when I was fifteen, Mama took a weeklong vacation to Marco Island, Florida. She went alone, staying at a Marriott beach resort. She flew back through Miami, where she stopped off to visit my paternal grandparents. Grandma Catherine said the time away had been good for Mama's spirits.

When she returned, Mama announced that she'd cashed in her Marriott stock and put a down payment on a house. That Sunday morning, when she said she'd been approved for the mortgage, I broke down in tears. I assumed she would be moving back to St. Louis County without me. I thought that only reasonable, given what our lives had been. She was scheduled to close the loan that Monday, she said. The owner was Ted Smith, the man Mama had rented from in St. Ann.

"Pack your things," my mother said. "When I get back from signing the papers at Mr. Smith's office, we need to go buy you a new mattress and a bed frame."

I started jumping, flailing my arms, screaming "Hallelujah!" over and over again like I did in church.

Until that moment, I had not let myself believe that I missed living with my mother. I had no idea what the new house even looked like. I just knew it was ours. I stomped so hard the floorboards shifted beneath my feet.

Auntie Gerald's voice boomed from downstairs, "Who that beating on my dern floor?"

Out of breath, I laughed and cried in Mama's arms on the bathroom floor. She smiled and stroked away my tears.

25

We moved into a small white house on Stanwood Drive off Bermuda Road and I-70, a quick shot up the highway to her job. She put in paperwork to get me into the school desegregation program. The slots were full, but the superintendent scanned my report cards and decided I was the kind of student they wanted. They sent a cab driver to pick me up every morning until a new stop on the long bus route was established.

I quickly settled back in with old friends and joined them in tenth grade at Ritenour Senior High School. This time, Mama helped me pick out my classes and decided I should take a theater elective and an extra writing class. She warned me to choose my friends carefully. My mother never had to say Black, but I knew what she meant. There were kids from Elmwood and Brentwood, two predominantly Black neighborhoods in the Ritenour district. The desegregation program meant there would be more kids from down in the city.

It was the first time I had experienced an even marginally integrated school. It had always been one or the other,
all Black or all white. Traversing the divide, on top of every
other complication of high school life, was rough. I quickly
mastered the art of code-switching, changing how I talked
and even walked, depending on who else was around.

I heard Kenneth's voice in my head.

Never let where you are become who you are.

That Christmas, I flew back to Miami to visit my grandparents. We went to a holiday party hosted by Grandpa
Roy's fraternity, the Boule, at a country club. Grandma Cat
dressed me in tuxedo pants, a blouse and patent leather kitten heels. She dabbed a bit of makeup on my face and clipped
my hair. Grandpa wore a white suit and a black dress shirt.
Cat swooped her hair up in a bun and slipped on a glorious
formfitting black sequined gown.

Though my grandparents hadn't mentioned it, there had
been another riot, this time in 1982, after Miami police shot
a Black man. The incident took place in a video arcade in
Overtown, a short distance from my grandparents' house.
When I asked my grandfather about it, he reminded me that
I was to stay inside their front fence. A boy around the way
was sweet on me, he said, but I shouldn't look his way.

"He isn't going to get sweet on anything but my broom,"
Grandma Cat said. "My brilliant child. Look at you. Your
father would be so proud."

That night at the ball, a horse jockey, a man no bigger than me, regaled us with stories about his races around the world while Judge Thomas and his wife, Jeannie, danced under a strobe light. Those were happy moments, watching my grandparents mingle among their friends. At fifteen, I was the only child in the room.

"There are great expectations for you," Mrs. Thomas said. "I understand you like James Baldwin."

"Yes, ma'am."

A few days later, before we left for the airport, Mrs. Thomas came over with a gift. I finished reading *The Fire Next Time* before the turn of the New Year.

Our little house had two small bedrooms adjoined by a short hallway. Mama bought furniture from a hotel salvage sale and went about tastefully decorating the rooms. It was half the size of Auntie Gerald's house but, for the first time in her life, my mother had the keys to a property that belonged to her. She had a second key cut at the hardware store and handed it to me. Surrounded by a friendly pack of neighbors, I didn't have to hide my growing library of books in anybody's closet. It was good to feel at home.

At school, I was reunited with my old friends from Buder and Hoech. The district, once predominantly white, had begun to integrate due to a statewide desegregation mandate. Black kids were bused to the suburban enclave, sometimes boarded in the predawn hours. Still, the racial lines remained, and I'd need to navigate the divide. It was generally harmonious. Though, I was one of the few kids who moved easily between both worlds.

It was too late to join the speech and debate teams. I'd missed concert choir tryouts, too. As a consolation, Mama enrolled me in a drama class where I learned the rigors of improv and method acting.

"Give it some time," Mama cautioned. "You won't be the star of every show."

She'd never been around to help select my academic schedule before and she seemed to revel in the idea now.

"You did so well at Rock," she said. "If you stay focused, you can go to any college you want."

It was the first time my mother ever mentioned anything beyond a high school diploma. She wanted to read my essays and sometimes watched me practice reciting plays in the kitchen.

Now working as front desk manager at the Marriott, during one of her shifts, she'd met a man who worked for Howard University in Washington, DC. Dr. William Sherrill was dean of admissions and financial aid. He was staying in the hotel for a few days and Mama said he wanted to meet me.

After hot combing my hair and wrapping it in a ballerina ball, she gathered up my report cards and a photo album full of awards. I put on a dressy skirt and blouse. We drove to the hotel and waited in the lobby for him to arrive. Mama needed special permission from the general manager to talk to hotel guests outside of work. He'd gleefully agreed, telling my mother what a great opportunity it was.

"Your mother says you are something special," Dean Sherrill said. "You belong at Howard."

He promised Mama that if I stayed the course, the institution would make sure my tuition was taken care of. I watched my mother beat back tears.

Not long after school started back, after the holiday break in January 1984, my mother got the call we'd been dreading. Uncle Ross had already suffered a heart attack, at least two major strokes and a string of transient ischemic attacks, or ministrokes. Now, paramedics were fighting to revive him.

"Hurry on," Grandma Alice said. "The ambulance done come. They upstairs working on him."

Uncle Ross had been bedridden for months, unable to climb the stairs or perform routine functions on his own. His left side completely paralyzed, his arm bound up in a sling, he struggled to feed himself. But what I will remember most was my uncle's emotional pain, and how the mourning seemed to engulf their house even before he drew his last breath.

As he suffered through those final months, his body and spirit thinning, he started rejecting his medications in an attempt to hasten his own death. Rather than swallowing the scheduled doses my aunt gave him, he hid them in his cheeks and spit them out. In the bottom of the wastebasket, we found tablets of various shapes, colors and sizes.

"Lord Jesus, take me away from here," I'd heard him say that Thanksgiving. "Take me home."

They were happy people, my aunt and uncle, coupled and fully in love until the day he died from a stroke that took the light out of his eyes. The truth is, though, notwithstanding that third stroke or some other catastrophic medical incident, my uncle likely could have persisted in his diminished state for many years. Whether or not physical therapy would have been even modestly effective long-term is not known. We do know that he was experiencing an inordinate level of pain, both physically and mentally, and that he wanted to die.

Grandma Alice said he was marking time.

I wanted to watch him paint the house again. I missed the precise way he would supreme an orange, separating its thin inner skins from the meaty sections. He was a simple man with pedantic tastes, who nevertheless lived elegantly.

Unable to speak or move on his own volition, Uncle Ross was now wasting away on the same roll-out bed where my mother and I had slept. He had moved about the planet on his own power and now he was choosing to leave it the same way. Without the aid of the prescribed blood-thinning medication, which he spit out almost as soon as we left the room, a new blood clot formed, and he suffered another major stroke.

We sped down I-70 through St. Louis, across the Mississippi River and into Illinois. By the time we got to the house that night, he was gone. Booky met me at the edge of the curb. Together we cried under the light post.

We sat on the porch swing that night, laughing, crying and telling old stories about the things we thought we'd gotten away with.

"It was his time, Go Go," Booky said.

The hurt was so intense, so thorough and complete, I began

to wail, and my sobs turned to yelps then whimpers. Mama ran to the porch and took hold of me with both arms.

"Give him back!" I cried. "Give him back!"

"Grief," as Joan Didion wrote so eloquently in *The Year of Magical Thinking*, "turns out to be a place none of us know until we reach it."

Albert Ross died on January 31, 1984. According to his obituary, he was fifty-seven years old.

That summer, Mama was back working nights again. She had been promoted to manage Marriott's rooftop restaurant and dressed more conservatively now. She stopped wearing wigs and fake eyelashes, preferring her own hair and her own way about life. My mother was home more often, but I was still largely on my own. She let me get a job at a movie theater near Northwest Plaza, where I scooped popcorn and ran the soda machine.

With the money I saved from running the concession stand at a movie theater at Northwest Plaza and with help from my godfather, Thom Puckett, I bought an IBM Selectric typewriter. I used it to draft a manuscript. I titled it: *Wade in the Water: Essays on Race and Poverty in America*.

In one piece, entitled "Somebody Oughta Say Something," I castigated state and local leaders over public corruption, environmental justice, the decision to move state police into East St. Louis, and what I called the warehousing of children in a failed public education system. I pointed out that white, former city leaders conspired with the state to move the city's boundaries, de-annexing a large swath, creating the new city of Sauget and stripping East St. Louis of its economic base.

I started and never finished my first novel, *Ghost River*. It was set in East St. Louis during the 1917 massacre. The research led me to start tracing our family history through the Deep South and our traditions back to the shores of West Africa and Haiti, where our ancestors were first enslaved, to examine the customs that both enlivened and haunted us.

When white workers went on strike at Aluminum Ore Company, the management brought in African Americans to replace them. It is said that more than 250 Black people were killed in the three-day crisis, though the official death toll is just thirty-nine, nine of them white people. Six thousand Black people were burned out of their homes. Whiskey Chute, a south end neighborhood that was once lined with fancy restaurants and bars that served the factory workers and hog skinners, went down in flames. I typically stayed up writing well into the night, plied with cups of Mama's Sanka.

After I hounded the coach, flashing my medals, I was allowed to join the competitive speech and debate team at Ritenour Senior High, then at Normandy, where I later transferred in my junior year. I still liked competing and winning was intoxicating. But I'd found my voice on the page. I worked and reworked lines of poetry until I heard them singing in my head.

With my sixteenth birthday around the corner, Mama taught me how to drive in her Pontiac T-1000. Puckett purchased a '74 Ford Mustang from the auto auction. It cost six hundred dollars and needed some repairs, including a rear spring, a distributor cap, brake pads, a new battery and a set of good tires. Puckett and Uncle Frank worked on it in his shop. When it was ready, Mama drove me down to his Sinclair gas station. He emerged from the bay with a broad, toothy smile.

"Come on over here and get a look at it."

He waved me into the garage. It was seafoam green, inside and out, just like Auntie Gerald's house. Uncle Frank wheeled it out to a pump, filled it with gasoline and tossed me the keys.

Puckett, who gifted me that bike in 1980, warned me to be careful about who I allowed into the passenger seat. He admonished me never to let anybody else drive it, especially Donnie.

"Keep this tank full," he said. "You don't want to run out of gas and get stuck somewhere. It you get low, pull up to the pump and Frank will fill you up."

Then, just as now, I wanted everybody to see my new car.

I drove myself to work at Northwest Plaza that Friday night. When the shift was over and I finished shoveling popcorn into oversize plastic bags for storage, I collected my paycheck. I went up to my mother's job, where I signed it over to her. She gave me the cash in exchange and deposited the check into her bank account. At $3.35 an hour minus taxes, it was a little over fifty dollars. I wanted to know who FICA was and why she got money out of my paycheck. Mama laughed.

"I'm going to spend the night with Rachel," I said, referring to one of my new friends.

Rachel was on the "de-seg" program and took the bus to school.

"Tell Mrs. Lane I said hello."

It was a lie.

I cut out of the hotel parking lot and got on the entryway ramp to I-70 westbound. It was late. The roads grew darker as I tooled along listening to Magic 108 until the audio got fuzzy and I lost the signal. I found a country music station, rolled down the windows, lit a cigarette and kept going.

It was a two-hour drive, and I arrived in Columbia, Missouri, sometime after midnight. Without a map, I drove around looking for Valley Mobile Park. A police officer at a stoplight pointed me down the road and around a bend.

"It's on the left-hand side," he said.

Kenneth lived off campus and worked part-time as an usher at university events. I hadn't called him first and the lights were out in the trailer. Figuring he had to come back at some point, I sat in the dark and waited until I fell asleep. The headlights woke me up.

"Goldie?"

"Hey."

"You're here?"

"I am."

He drew me in, placed his palms on my face, and kissed me on the forehead.

"So, you'd still rather have you mind, than a cute behind?"

"I was going to tell you," he said. "But I have a girlfriend now."

"You do?"

He nodded and hugged me.

"Come on inside," he said. "It's raining."

EPILOGUE: CRY LIKE A RAINY DAY

More than anything, I think she simply needs somebody to listen. Daily phone calls with my mother are often littered with her tears. She complains of being overwhelmed and, at eighty, she is confused over the most routine matters. She is still haunted, I know, by my father's murder. Her weather-beaten skin seems to have darkened with the years and she's racked up emotional maladies that assault her sense of balance. It is the trauma, I know, bottled up and undiluted.

Grief, they say, is love with nowhere to go.

Though it spanned a mere seven years, the tumultuous relationship, at times beautiful and at others marred with animosity and violence, left an indelible mark on her psyche. More than four decades after my father's murder, the memories of the man who loved my mother with an unbridled ferocity are both a pain and a refuge that she alone can know. While she has largely chosen silence to cope with his absence, over the years she has wondered aloud, as I sometimes do, what our lives might have been.

It was Toni Morrison who said, "The love is never any better than the lover. Wicked people love wickedly, violent people love violently, weak people love weakly, stupid people love stupidly."

When it comes to my father, my mother speaks mostly of the joys and almost never of the sorrows. She leaves out the wicked, violent, and stupid. As a young woman, she was never the kind to wear her disappointments, preferring instead a fresh slick of lipstick, a whiff of cleavage, showgirl eyelashes and knee-high go-go boots. I suppose I inherited her sense of resilience, her steadiness amid tumult, if not her proclivity for sequined ball gowns, spaghetti strap stilettos and lash extensions. Like my mother, I've been a platinum blonde one time too many. Similarly, we are sometimes untrusting, cynical creatures, yet empathetic and benevolent in ways that sometimes leave our spiritual and physical storehouses empty.

Two years ago, I invited her over for dinner. I was doing more cooking than usual and she was eager to help me empty a pan of roasted salmon, blood oranges and fennel. She was never much of a cook, but my mother and I enjoy food like a second religion.

She came toting a stack of months-old mail that hadn't been forwarded by the post office. It had been better than twenty-five years since I lived in that house, though my name is still on the mortgage and, like most things, I never quite got around to renewing the change of address. As I sorted through the pile of outdated coupons and various solicitations, my mother drew a thick envelope from her handbag.

"These are from your father."

A ball of air caught in the bend of my throat. I stared down at the marble kitchen countertop. What could be said now, I wondered; after all, he was her husband, not mine. I had not lain with him at night or readied his dinners. I had not birthed his child or taken in another who wasn't my own, nor had I paced the floors when he didn't come home at night. He had not blacked my eye, stalked me for years on end, or shoved my face through a plate-glass window. I had not been forced to identify his body, selected his funeral clothes or chosen the cemetery where they put him in the ground. I had not prayed over him like I was down to my last slice of bread.

"I thought you might want to read them," she said. "I made copies."

I could not look at her. I could not touch the letters.

"Do you want to read them?"

I nodded.

After dinner, I put away the dishes, and opened the floor-to-ceiling blinds to reveal the starless sky. I poured two more glasses of wine—a Pinot Noir I knew my mother had grown fond of. We kicked off our shoes and settled onto the sofa.

"He would be proud of you," she said.

I offered her my bed but, as always, she chose the oversize sectional sofa. Ellington and Coltrane streamed through the speakers in the ceiling. Lulled by a third and arguably unnecessary glass of wine, she curled up in her favorite corner and dozed off. I covered her with a quilt and watched her sleep.

★ ★ ★

Auntie Gerald got sick again last week. At eighty-six, she was in the health one might expect, and well beyond the years when self-examination might have proven more worthwhile. She fell unconscious and Fat Man, now in his forties, called for an ambulance. She was unresponsive, but still breathing, amid end-state congenital heart failure. Her kidneys were failing, and she had pneumonia in her left lung. Paramedics intubated her.

"It's a waiting game now," Mama said.

I fell on my knees and prayed. I made a deal with God. I wanted to hear her voice.

"And, if ain't too much trouble," I said, "let her say my name."

Ronnie Lee, now on in age and beset with his own health issues, was allowed into the intensive care unit. Someone needed to sign the order to remove the ventilator. Once she was stable, Auntie Gerald was released and sent home to hospice.

"We got the hospital bed last night, she got blood in her urine now," Mama said. "Don't know how long it will be now. It's so hard to see her like this. Bug doing all she can. I can't stop crying, my heart so full. She is responsive, eyes barely open and she very weak. She tries to talk. You can barely make it out."

Last night, in what would be her final hours, lulled by pain medication and unable open her eyes, she called my name.

"Goldie, I'll see you after-while," she whispered.

I went to bed thinking about the porch swing and how

Auntie used to sit up in the shade and admire the rosebushes Uncle Ross planted for her. The house is now in disrepair. Weeds spring from the cracks in the asphalt and shroud the faces of the few abandoned houses still standing along the block.

Auntie Gerald passed on this morning. Mama called, wondering if I could start writing the obituary. Gerald kept notes about what she wanted said and done when she went home to see Jesus. She left a lengthy list of spirituals and specific instructions about how she wants to be laid to rest. Her handwriting, like the love she gave, is unsteady and imperfect.

If you look at a thing long enough, good, bad, or otherwise, you can see God in it.

Survivors look back and see things they missed, things that escaped them in the moments of stillness or when the world spun too furiously. There are burdens that I believed were my obligation to carry in silence. For far too many years, I lived life as if holding my breath.

A thin brown keloid runs along my right heel from when it was sliced open by a broken bottle in that Duck Hill public housing project. A faint blemish on the back of my right hand is where the tip of an electric iron burned away the skin that same year. There are calluses from swinging hammers, digging ditches, and holding on to life too tightly. My knuckles are still dented from schoolyard fistfights and scrapping with cousins.

"Love does not begin and end the way we seem to think it does," Baldwin wrote in *Nobody Knows My Name: More*

Notes of a Native Son. "Love is a battle; love is a war; love is a growing up."

In our family, and I suppose in others, love came with a taste of war. It was in the pushing and pulling, planting, and harvesting, chasing children away from an open fire hydrant and making sure they all get home before the streetlights come on. It sounded like Sandy Farrell calling her Richard in from the yard and him and his boys hauling in the groceries. It was Wendell Goins, the retired firefighter, who made house with his schoolteacher wife and put all his seven children, including Kenneth, through college.

Love sounded like clanging pots, smelled like Sunday dinner after an hours-long sermon, the roar of a vacuum cleaner across my Auntie Gerald's red carpets and plucking weeds from the yard. It was my Uncle Ross's set of encyclopedias, bought on time payments, and the rabbit coat he ordered her from a catalog. It was waiting out the rain to hang the laundry on the line. It was pressing out his pants, like Auntie Killer did for Uncle Willie Byrd, pushing him to get sober and letting him keep that toothpick in his mouth for family photographs. For Mama, it was Daddy pulling Lori Ann in from a tornado before the winds swept her little body away. It was also tucking away the pain to give him the respect of a burial.

For Auntie Gerald, I know, it was soothing his cracked lips with a damp cloth and some balm, long after he cannot recall your name. It was washing down his ashen, browning skin and slicking petroleum jelly on his knees and elbows, long after other people stopped coming by to see how he was making it day to day. It was opening your doors to a broken little girl who needed somebody to watch over her.

I am reminded now of something else Baldwin said.

"And once you realize that you can do something, it would be difficult to live with yourself if you didn't do it," he wrote in the *Paris Review*.

I sometimes wonder what I might have been, but for the puss and scarring of sexual violence and how it formed and defined and confined me. But, if suffering breeds perseverance and defines character, given the choice, I might have traded endurance for a heart that beats evenly. Mostly, though, I want to love better.

★ ★ ★ ★ ★

ABOUT THE AUTHOR

Goldie Taylor is a veteran journalist, cable news political analyst and human rights activist. Currently a contributing editor at the *Daily Beast*, where she writes about national politics and social justice issues, Taylor has been a working journalist for over thirty-five years. She got her start as a staff writer at the *Atlanta Journal-Constitution* and as a desk assistant with CBS News Atlanta. Today, she is also senior vice president and chief communications and marketing officer at Dana-Farber Cancer Institute.

The former television news and communications executive has been featured on nearly every major network—including NBC News, MSNBC, ABC News, CNN and HLN—and she has been a guest on programs such as HBO's *Real Time with Bill Maher*, *The Dr. Phil Show*, *The Steve Harvey Show*, and *Good Morning America*. Taylor is a frequent guest on a full host of local and national radio shows, including NPR's *All Things Considered*, and has been regularly published in print and digital publications. In recent years, she has written dozens of guest op-ed columns for *Salon*, *Atlanta Journal-Constitution*, *Creative Loafing*, *St. Louis Post-Dispatch*, *TheGrio*, *Huffington Post*, CNN.com, MSNBC.com, and *Essence* among others.

In November 2015, Taylor penned the cover story for *Ebony Magazine* about the legacy of comedic icon Bill Cosby and made a cameo appearance on BET's *Being Mary Jane*. She was a contributing producer for "CNN Presents: The Atlanta Child Murders" and has been an executive consultant to the presidents of both NBC News and CNN Worldwide.

A sought-after public speaker, Taylor has addressed audiences at—among others—the National Center for Civil and Human Rights, Harvard University, Morehouse College, Emory School of Law, Princeton University, Duke School of Law, National Association of Black Journalists, University of Missouri School of Journalism and The King Center.

A somewhat less than devoted runner, late blooming golfer, and self-professed connoisseur of mediocre whiskey, Taylor has three grown children and three grandchildren. She lives in Boston and is wholly convinced that "God has a sense of humor."

ACKNOWLEDGMENTS

I want to thank my daughter Katie Wingate, whose gentle encouragement set me on this path, and my son, Joshua Taylor, who served as my spiritual guardian when I lost my balance along the way. If I thanked you both a thousand times a day for a thousand years, it would never be enough. To my editor, John Glynn, and literary agent, Eve Attermann, you have my deepest appreciation for lending me your stewardship and patience, and for giving me the space to have my say. And, finally, to my granddaughter, Taylor-Marie, the blessings you bring to my life number the stars. I am most grateful for the gift of your presence and for the opportunity to love more than I ever believed possible.